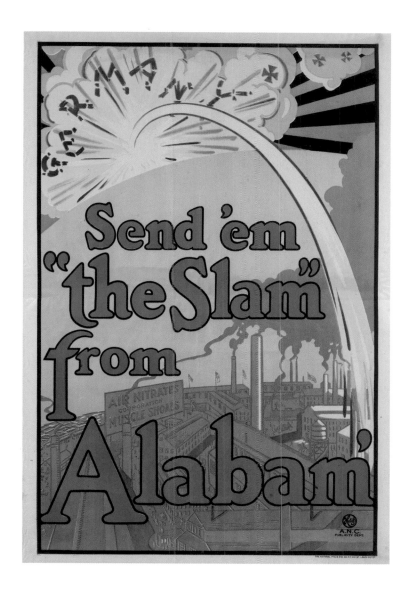

WHICH

OUGHT <u>YOU</u> TO WEAR?

Issued by the Publicity Dept., Central London Recruiting Depôt. Whitehall. S.W.

Printed by Sir Joseph Causton & Sons. Ltd., 9, Eastcheap. E C

James Aulich

War Posters

WEAPONS OF MASS COMMUNICATION

Thames & Hudson

With 329 illustrations, 303 in color

PAGE 1
August William (Angiet) Hutaf
Send 'em "the slam" from Alabam' 1917, USA

PAGE 2
Unknown
Which ought you to wear? 1914, UK

PAGE 5, LEFT TO RIGHT
H. Devitt Welsh,
They give their lives. Do you lend your savings? c.1918, USA

Gerald Spencer Pryse
Belgian Red Cross Fund 1915, UK

Ferdy Horrmeyer
Vote Socialist 1919, Germany

John Atherton
A careless word ... another cross 1943, USA

Jamie Reid
Peace is tough 2003, UK

First published in 2007 in hardcover in the United States of America by Thames & Hudson Inc., 500 Fifth Avenue, New York, New York 10110

thamesandhudsonusa.com

Library of Congress Catalog Card Number 2007901210

ISBN 978-0-500-25141-6

Printed in Singapore by C S Graphics Pte Ltd

Acknowledgments

This book, and the exhibition it accompanies, arose from a collaborative project between the Manchester Institute for Research and Innovation in Art and Design (MIRIAD) at Manchester Metropolitan University (MMU) and the Imperial War Museum (IWM) in London. A combination of scholarly, historical and curatorial expertise contributed to the cataloguing and publication on the web of 10,000 posters. The larger part of this internationally significant resource is now open to academic, curatorial and general audiences for the first time.

The project received institutional and financial support from the Arts and Humanities Research Council (AHRC), the IWM and MIRIAD. Particular thanks must go to individuals who have unstintingly given of their support and expertise. At the IWM: Angela Weight, Michael Moody, Kathleen Palmer, Richard Slocombe and Dill Banerjee who provided additional photography, as well as the project team Sarah Holt, Richard Slocombe (again), Robin Blackburn, Rosalyn Scott and Andy Green. At MMU: John Hewitt, Professor John Hyatt and members of the Visual Culture Research Centre.

Help with the extended captions was provided by Richard Slocombe and Michael Moody, and welcome editorial advice was received from Liz Bowers and Terry Charman at the IWM, and Rebeka Cohen at Thames & Hudson. Thanks also to Sarah Praill for the design. But most of all I would like to thank my wife Lynn for her loving support, and the indulgence of our two children, Alice and John, in getting this book to press.

Using their unique reference numbers (which can be found in the illustration list at the back of the book), many of the posters included in this publication can be accessed through the Imperial War Museum website www.iwm.org.uk or on the AHDS Visual Arts database www.vads.ahds.ac.uk

Contents

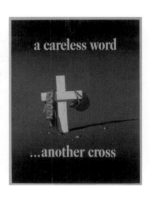

Peter Kennard   1   **Untitled (Poster Number 1, Stop the War Coalition)** 2003
UK

Introduction

The posters reproduced and discussed in this book are drawn from the largest and most comprehensive collection of its type in existence. They were published by governmental organizations, political parties, commercial concerns, charities, non-governmental organizations and protest or special-interest groups. As instruments for promoting and disseminating war aims, social cohesion, ideological purpose and various forms of citizenship, and in more recent times for voicing opposition, these posters document the social, political, ethnic and cultural aspirations of belligerent nations involving Britain and the Empire from the First World War to the present day.

The First World War posters were systematically collected and the most exhaustive analysis relates to them. The IWM's collection was substantially added to in the Second World War but did not receive much attention until the appointments of Michael Moody as Research and Information Officer, and Angela Weight as Keeper of the Department of Art, in the 1970s.

L. R. Bradley, Keeper of War Publicity at the IWM, first established the collection in 1917, and it included cartoons, advertisements, show cards, proclamations and other printed ephemera, as well as official posters. The collection was intended as an encyclopaedic record of the war's impact on popular visual commercial culture and as evidence of the impact of total war on everyday life. In this ambition, Bradley unwittingly preserved the wider visual discourses of posters that continue to give them meaning today.

The discovery that, even before the First World War had ended, the museum had amassed over 20,000 items, of which posters were only a part, stimulated a methodological approach that challenges the aesthetic view of the poster as an autonomous medium. Bradley was never in pursuit of the beautiful poster: he was far more interested in the broader visual environment of daily experience. Inspired by Bradley's work, this book adopts a similar methodological approach that aims to explore the poster in the context of wider debates concerning propaganda, publicity and advertising in relation to the media and modernity.

1

The poster, propaganda and publicity

PROPAGANDA AND OUTDOOR ADVERTISING

Ideally, the best posters are striking, economical and efficient, and deliver a direct and simple message. Often, the public information poster will struggle for hearts and minds, and will warn of duplicitous counter-propaganda from the enemy in order to stir the nation to action. As a psychological weapon deployed on home ground, propagandists recognized the importance of inspiring the individual to action by whatever means possible: 'They shall not pass!', for example, depicted what the Germans called a 'peace offensive' during the First World War as an unexploded shell (3).

Deployed by agencies whose best interests were served by alternately bewitching, terrifying and beguiling the public, these posters urged, cajoled, seduced and coerced. They were, and are, part of a popular cultural landscape over which the general public has little control. They still litter our urban environment and public spaces and assault us with bright colours and loud typography. Yet paradoxically they are frequently proclaimed to be *the* democratic medium.

Governments first adopted the techniques of advertising during the First World War, establishing shifting and symbiotic relationships with both commercial culture and the media industry. Under these conditions, the relationships between the producers and their public can be more important than the symbolisms, messages and directives of the posters themselves. More significantly, by working with the government, the advertising trade gained a respectability and legitimacy it had previously lacked.

The Mayor of Westminster makes a public appeal for war bonds in Trafalgar Square, London, 1917.

Maurice Neumont **3** **They shall not pass!** 1918
France

During the First World War in Britain, Charles Higham, one of the first champions of publicity, claimed that posters improved lives by informing the public of new products, modes of behaviour and even appearance. Advances in transport, hygiene, diet and labour-saving devices were understood to broaden the moral and aesthetic horizons of the nation. But his view was by no means unique. In January 1919 'The Londoner' in the *Evening News* cast a favourable light on Bolshevik posters because of their educative role, while a book published by the Outdoor Advertising Association of America in 1925 quoted from a sermon given to the trade in Westminster Abbey, London, by the Bishop of Durham, Dr Hensley Henson. In this speech, Henson described the poster as a persuasive and positive educational force that provided social and aesthetic frameworks, much as religious art had done in the past.

The poster is the exemplary modern medium and it appeals to the most modern of phenomena, the masses. In the early 20th century, psychologists such as Walter Dill Scott and Gustave Le Bon believed the masses to be susceptible to contagious and irrational suggestion through the subconscious and by the affirmation and repetition of appealing statements. They understood that the masses might be vulnerable to exploitation by demagogues, but these doubts were outweighed by the perceived benefits of the efficient delivery of information offered by the poster.

In his book *Propaganda*, published in 1928, an American champion of publicity, Edward L. Bernays, spoke of an informed and invisible ruling elite in democratic societies that manipulated public opinion and controlled the masses. And as early as 1922 the well-known liberal and pacifist philosopher Bertrand Russell warned of what his fellow philosopher Noam Chomsky would later refer to as 'the manufacture of consent' in his book, *Necessary Illusions*, when he wrote about American monopolies whose influence he compared to that of the Soviet state. Russell also drew attention to an education system that churned out literate but uncritical young people influenced by absurd propaganda claims derived from the art of advertising. By the time of the start of the Second World War, the American writer and journalist Clark Blake had recognized the widespread identification of national purpose with commerce and consumerism, noting that a literal reading of advertising would give as much credit for victory in Italy in 1945 to Pepsi and Coca Cola as it would to the armed services.

3 Opposite
Published by an organization dedicated to countering German propaganda, this poster warns French civilians not to trust any peace overtures from the hypocritical *Boche* after their second defeat on the Marne (18 July to 7 August 1918).

Unknown **4** Terrorists? You have seen them. Are you going
to tell the authorities about them? 2003
Iraq

4 Above
This poster urges co-operation with the
occupying forces and the Iraqi interim
government in southern Iraq.

5 Opposite
Toscani did not feature Benetton
merchandise in his advertising campaigns
for this fashion label, choosing to address
social issues instead. In this case, a real-
life photograph of Albanian refugees
fleeing by boat from Kosovo is the
backdrop to this poster.

The poster is also the most modern of media because
it is integral to the urban environment. Placed adjacent to
entertainment venues, by railway lines and along main urban
routes, posters were in the commercial hearts, industrial centres,
public squares and transport hubs of cities around the world.
They adorned the trams, buses and taxis in order to catch the
average four-second gaze of the traveller. The modern man and
woman were their targets: shoppers, office workers, managers,
artisans and labourers.

The appeal of the hoarding for the advertiser is as strong
today as it was in the early 20th century. Despite a fall in the
number of sites dedicated to hoardings, there has been a steady
growth in expenditure on outdoor advertising, and billboards
are permanently on display to all who pass by. Indeed, in many
countries, the explosion of unsightly hoardings has frequently
led to self-regulation and legislation in order to restrict their
number and control their content.

According to a report produced in 2002 for the Advertising
Standards Authority in the UK, the public ranked posters
second only to television advertising in impact. As a source
of information and a form of communication, entertainment
and culture, posters play a part in everyday life and contribute
to a popular visual landscape: they function as landmarks and
diversions for commuters; they are topics of conversation and
can introduce difficult subjects, such as the War on Terror, or,
as in the past, duty to King and Country; and they help to
shape attitudes to everything from the latest style accessory
to religious and ethnic stereotyping.

Advertising posters could be argued to serve no intentional
social or cultural purpose beyond broadcasting the existence
of a product and the merchandising of a lifestyle. Yet as a
compensation for their uninvited presence, they often entertain,
despite being no more profound than the cereal packet on
the breakfast table. Unlike the cereal packet, however, the non-
commercial poster is a vehicle for government information and
special-interest groups. Such posters provide the visual rhetoric
behind the implementation of, or opposition to, government
policy. Especially in times of political or social upheaval, posters
can become calls to action, and can inform and influence
behaviour in ways that guide the public towards a particular
political ideology.

In the officially sponsored public information poster,
advertising experts bridge the gap between government and
people. More often than not, this type of poster depicts its
target audience as its producers would most like to envisage
it, reality aside. And yet these posters often contain much more
than surface appearance or obvious messages. Their production,

consumption and reception in the aesthetic, social, political and geographical contexts that give them meaning, help to reveal the relationships between governments, advertising and commerce, propaganda and the public. As the American Germanophile and propagandist G. S. Viereck put it in his book *Spreading Germs of Hate* (1931): 'Americans were the best propagandists because they were the best advertisers ... we called it politics, business, publicity, invisible government. We did not label it propaganda.'

In Western liberal democracies, public information and propaganda posters are part of the advertising industry, yet the industry's all-pervasiveness sometimes serves to make posters all the more invisible. Charity appeals, corporate image campaigns and cause-related publicity can create propaganda specifically to manipulate emotional response without offering any rational discussion. Interestingly, according to the UK Advertising Standards Authority, the most popular billboard posters were humorous ones, and those where a style statement passes for engagement (5). Their purpose is to get people to buy, not to stir them to action.

The ambiguity of pictorial imagery can as easily divide as unite a nation. In Germany during the First World War, the military's own market research showed that spectacular Wagnerian imagery failed to connect with the people, but they continued to produce it nonetheless. By way of contrast, in France at the same time, posters also driven by government policy featured Republican imagery that for all its allegorical pomposity drew upon a tradition that resonated with the French people.

But this is only part of the story. In Canada, Herbert A. Williams writing for *The Poster War Souvenir Issue* in 1920 remarked that posters had infiltrated dignified conservative businesses, churches, monuments of historical significance and public areas that were previously off-limits to commercial culture. What was inappropriate for high bourgeois institutions and civic spaces suddenly became acceptable in the context of the physical and financial sacrifices demanded by government war aims. The vocabulary of commercialism – through the techniques of advertising – reached into respectable middle- and working-class lives formerly resistant to the marketplace.

For a more contemporary example, it is enlightening to look at Iraq since the 2003 invasion. The Iraqi government, occupation forces and the various competing religious and political factions have found a highly visible and powerful voice in the poster (4). Posters purveying the benefits of democracy, encouraging young Iraqis to join the police force or promoting non-governmental organizations or the Red Cross get torn down (6). The only unblemished posters depict the Imams. Printers previously

Oliviero Toscani 5 **United Colors of Benetton** 1993 Italy

6 Top

A boy peeling a poster featuring
a portrait of President Allawi from
a wall in Baghdad, Iraq, 2005.

7 Above

A poster by David Gentleman – on behalf
of the Stop the War Coalition – protesting
against the UK's involvement in Iraq.
Palace of Westminster, London, 2003.

controlled by the Ministry of Information are free to print
whatever the market demands, illustrating the lack of separation
between the forces of individual liberty, religion, democracy,
commerce, publicity and propaganda.

During times of revolution, civil disturbance and social
change, territories are claimed, and boundaries often defined,
by the distribution of posters, even if only for a short time.
Demonstrators against the 2003 invasion of Iraq occupied parks,
streets and squares across the world, and were heavily policed.

In June 2001 Brian Haw made camp opposite the Palace of
Westminster in London in protest against the sanctions on Iraq
imposed by the British government (7). In 2005 his semi-
permanent forty-metre display of posters, banners and other
ephemera provoked the British parliament to include legislation
in the Serious Organized Crime and Police Act prohibiting
unauthorized demonstrations within a kilometre of Parliament
Square. At the beginning of 2007, artist Mark Wallinger installed
'State Britain' at Tate Britain, London. It reproduced Haw's protest
as it had existed before the police removed it from outside the
Palace of Westminster in May 2006. Wallinger's installation
incorporated works donated to Haw's protest by graffiti artist
Banksy (8) and graphic artist Leon Kuhn (9), and illustrated the
involvement of artists with political activism and the techniques
of publicity in a tradition going back as far as Germany in 1919.
A line on the gallery floor marked the boundary of the exclusion
zone defined by government legislation that directly addresses
civil liberties, demarcation, power and freedom of speech.

In this case, what was intolerable in a public space was
accommodated by the state-owned but liberal space of the art
gallery. The culture of politics and the politics of culture are thus
divided. The US provided a mirror image example. The managers
of the Chelsea Market in New York removed Chris Savido's
portrait of George Bush from an exhibition. Subsequently,
anonymous donors paid for 'Bush Monkeys' to be posted on
a giant digital billboard (10). These examples demonstrate how
the dynamics of government, commerce, culture, special-interest
groups, the advertising trade and the control of public space
give the poster its meaning.

ICONIC IMAGES

Alfred Leete's recruiting poster (16) has attained iconic status
since its creation in 1914, a fact that has little to do with its
effectiveness as a recruiting tool: its direct and unequivocal
address to the viewer provided a pattern for other designers
to follow (Montgomery Flagg adapted it in his design for the
American Army (18) and Mauzan used it in the poster he created
to advertise the Italian war loan campaign) (17).

The image contributes to a popular visual language through repetition: instantly recognizable and effective, it has had a long and sustained life. It was even subverted in a poster opposing the Vietnam War in America in 1972 in which the pointing finger of admonition becomes the beckoning finger of death (19).

SYMBOLIC LANGUAGES

Posters need to be effective. Descriptive narrative techniques involving elaborate illustration and text will not always hit the mark, and so designers often opt for the direct appeal in other ways (11). Poster artists made use of metonymy, where a part or attribute stands for the whole, as a flag can stand for a nation, or a shoe can stand for a cobbler – take the bomb as a figure of war, for example (12, 20–22). This technique liberated the artist from the need to describe and, if well chosen, proved an efficient and effective way of getting a message across.

PROPAGANDA STORIES

Since the first quarter of the 20th century, photographs have had an increasingly important part to play in the design of posters. Dispersed in the media, many photographs quickly become iconic in an 'objectively real' visual shorthand.

One of the most famous examples is Joe Rosenthal's photograph of the flag-raising on Iwo Jima during the battle

8 Top
Mark Wallinger's 'State Britain'
– a reconstruction of Brian Haw's protest against the sanctions imposed on Iraq by the UK government in 2001 – is displayed here in Tate Britain, London, 2007.

9 Above
A view of his protest outside Parliament Square, London, by Brian Haw, 2006.

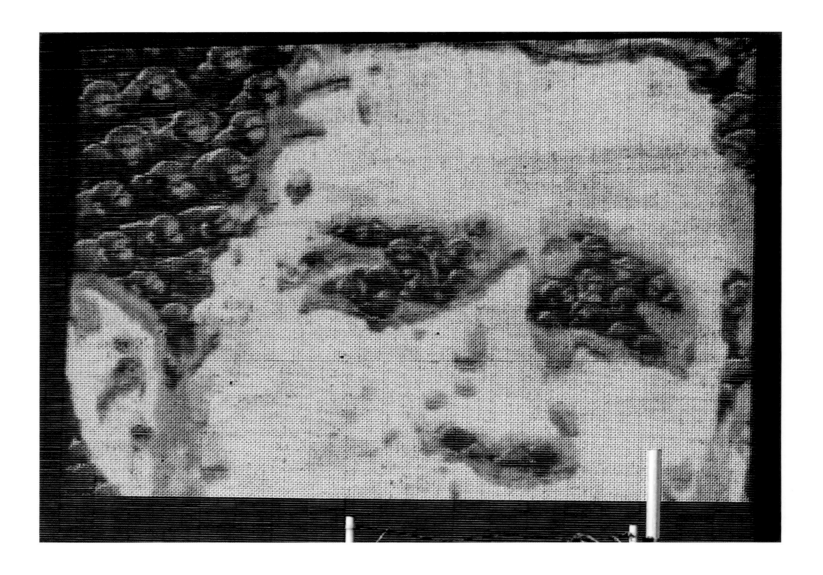

10 Above
Chris Savido's 'Bush Monkeys' portrait of US President George W. Bush, New York, 2004.

11 Opposite above
This poster was reproduced in James R. Mock and Cedric Larsen's *Words that Won the War*, 1939, with the caption 'Appeals to the lowest level of literacy and understanding'.

for the Pacific in the Second World War. Published widely in the press, it became an emblem of victory for a war-weary public. The magazine illustrator C. C. Beal painted it, and it was reproduced in a poster and re-enacted by the surviving participants during their national tour in the US Treasury's seventh war bonds drive in 1945. The fact that the photograph recorded a replacement flag, or that the battle still had several weeks to rage, or that one of the flag-raisers had been misidentified, was not allowed to interfere with the business of raising funds. Nor did it inhibit its use by Felix de Weldon as the basis for the US Marine Corps' memorial in Arlington Cemetery, or its re-enactment in the closing minutes of the John Wayne Hollywood film the *Sands of Iwo Jima* (1949).

The image has been re-used countless times. In 'Sarajevo Olympics' (14) its iconic status is used against itself to condemn the failure of the international community and the US to act against the Serbian nationalists who were shelling the city. Just as Kitchener admonishes as well as points with his finger, so the flag-raising is a raising of the cross.

Similarly, the controversial photographs of tortured Iraqis in Abu Ghraib prison in 2004 were universally distributed in the media around the world. They have provided valuable images for anti-war groups such the Stop the War Coalition who incorporated the photograph of the hooded prisoner into the design of one their posters (24). Again, this poster is not a simple objective record of an event: the outstretched arms are resonant of a supplicant Christ, so that the image is an indictment of Western traditions at the same time as recognizing the suffering of others.

Emotive images of atrocities involving prisoners and civilians are the stock in trade of the propagandist. In 1942 for example, Ben Shahn addressed the murder of civilians in an image that avoided graphic explicitness, but which at the same time conveyed a sense of menace (23). Atrocity propaganda was particularly vitriolic during the First World War and the British were its most effective exponents (26).

In the British press during the First World War, enemy atrocities were widely reported and sometimes quoted visually in recruiting posters. The British government published the internationally highly influential Bryce Report in 1915 that verified accounts of German murder and rape. Explicit images of atrocity were rare in this self-regulated trade, although less so in America where the Bryce Report played a crucial role in garnering support for the Allies: 'Your liberty bond will help stop this' (25) depicted a German soldier crucifying a Canadian soldier. The Bryce Committee had been lax in its terms of evidence and after the war this crucifixion story, which appeared in a number

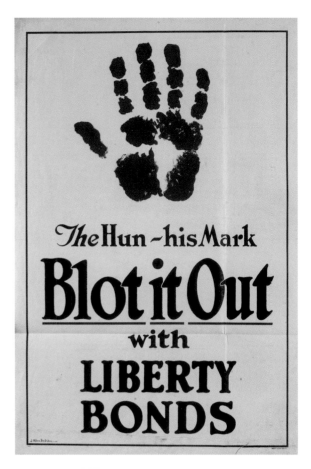

J. Allen St John 11 **Blot it out with liberty bonds** 1917
USA

Adolf Uzarski 12 **Like a bomb** 1918
Germany

Ellsworth Young  **13** **Remember Belgium** 1918
USA

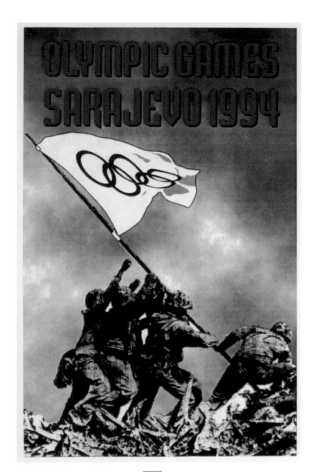

Dalida & Bojan HadÏilhalilovic, **14** **Sarajevo Olympics** 1994
Leila Hatt   Bosnia-Herzegovina

of different versions, was among many others shown to be unsubstantiated. Sadly, not all atrocities are fictional. In 1943 the mass graves of 5,000 Polish officers were discovered at Katyn near Smolensk in Russia, and a poster produced by the Nazis for occupied France (30) accurately placed the blame for the massacre on the NKVD (People's Commissariat for Internal Affairs, which was responsible for Stalin's foreign intelligence service and 'special operations').

Propriety and good taste have made rape a rare subject in posters until relatively recently (13, 28), although the victimization of women and children was a well-used theme for aid charities. Interpreted through the traditional Christian iconography of the *Pietà*, the image of a mother cradling a dead child in her arms became a symbol of cruelty, sacrifice and hope of resurrection. These images, some dating from the First World War, are familiar to us in contemporary popular culture via the photojournalistic reporting of the civilian suffering in Palestine, Darfur and Iraq. They confirm the strength of ancient compositional and iconographical schemes across temporal and political divides (30–32). The iconographical association with the Madonna and Child is also carried over into the highly emotive depiction of violated babies and children (27, 29, 33, 34).

RACIAL STEREOTYPING AND THE 'OTHER'
Another effective strategy in poster propaganda is the racial stereotyping of the enemy as aggressive, irrational and barbaric. Propriety tends to restrict images of this kind to less publicly visual media, such as the press and cartoons, novels, and in France during the first quarter of the 20th century, popular prints. Posters depicting the enemy as a race less than human and without moral qualities are in the minority, although they are not as scarce as those depicting graphic violence.

Germans are portrayed as barbarians: bestial, murderous and blood-drenched (35–37); the British are globe-consuming plutocratic John Bulls (40); and the Japanese are the slant-eyed, big-toothed and treacherous Yellow Peril with thick glasses (39). Occasionally, objectification goes so far as to represent the enemy as an animal. For example, the linguistic metaphor 'tentacles of power' was often interpreted visually as an octopus (15). Likewise, during the French and Belgian occupation of the Rhine and the Ruhr in the 1920s, French colonial troops from Africa were given exaggerated features and depicted as sexual predators (38): the message that negotiation with this irrational and subhuman other would be impossible was clear.

The degree of racist stereotyping evoked in 'Careless matches aid the Axis' (39), for example, is particularly disturbing as a representation of Japanese duplicity and as a vicious caricature of Japanese–Americans, of whom large numbers were interned by the authorities at the outbreak of hostilities in 1943. For all its effectiveness, the US Treasury's Second World War strategy of demonizing the Japanese as the Yellow Peril was afterwards sidelined in the interests of post-war racial harmony, peace and good business. Such racist discourse re-emerged during the wars with Korea and Vietnam to the extent that even one of the most respected anti-Vietnam war poster artists, Tomi Ungerer, was criticized for his unconsciously racist depictions of the Vietnamese as faceless ciphers (see 310 on page 239).

Another graphic strategy in posters, also familiar from the press cartoon, is the celebration and defacement of national, political and religious symbols. Broken, trodden swastikas (41–42) tellingly capture the sacrilegious nature of Nazi ideology. Unsurprisingly, the all-enveloping and triumphant national flag (44) is ubiquitous, while the Union flag captured by the German nation and distorted into the emblem of the heart – the symbol for charitable aid for German servicemen – is an eloquent subversion (43).

13 Opposite
The title of this American poster first appeared in British recruiting posters. According to the Germanophile propagandist G. S. Viereck, the implied theme of rape was designed to 'raise the blood of the American taxpayer to the boiling point and to lighten his pocket book' (*Spreading Germs of Hate*), and also to encourage Americans to invest in war savings.

14 Opposite
As the world looked on in 1994, Serbian Nationalist forces besieged Sarajevo during the Bosnian war. One of a series of posters that reworked Western cultural icons, this example was published during the siege and made ironic reference to the 1984 Winter Olympics, when Sarajevo was the centre of world attention for less infamous reasons.

15 Below
Designed by a British artist and distributed in the liberated South of the Netherlands, this poster concerned the Japanese occupation of Indonesia, and was published by the Dutch government-in-exile in London.

Pat Keely 15 The Indies shall be freed! 1944
UK

Alfred Leete 16 **Britons join your country's army!** 1914
UK

Personality Posters (after James Montgomery Flagg) 19 **I want you for US army** c.1972
UK

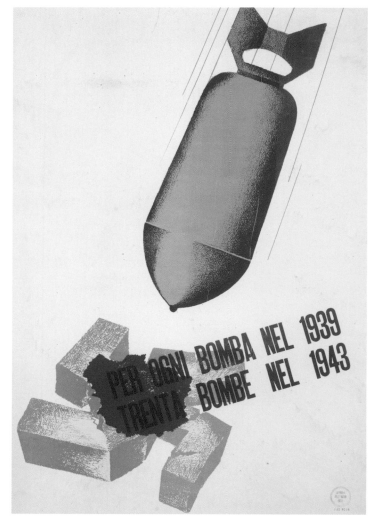

16 Page 20
This portrait of Lord Kitchener, hero of the Boer war and Secretary of State for War in 1914, originally appeared as a cover for the magazine *London Opinion*.

20 Above
The image of the bomb in this poster provides a forceful expression of the impact of 'More production' on the Nazis and the Japanese.

21 Above
In this poster the bomb crushes the Swastika both literally and symbolically.

22 Opposite
The photographic image of the Indochinese peasant combined with the 'op art' style and an overwhelmingly large bomb represents the scale of American air sorties over Cambodia during the Vietnam war.

Unknown **21** **For every bomb in 1939, thirty bombs in 1943** 1943
Italy

Within the poster:

A project of the Peoples Coalition for Peace and Justice

CAMPAIGN END THE AIR WAR   339 LAFAYETTE STREET   NEW YORK CITY   10012   (212) 777-5560

Design by David G. Bragin

UNDER NIXON
3 MILLION TONS
OF BOMBS
DROPPED ON
INDOCHINA

3 MILLION PEOPLE
KILLED, WOUNDED
OR HOMELESS

END THE AIR WAR

SET THE DATE
FOR COMPLETE
WITHDRAWAL

NO MORE AID
FOR THIEU

David G. Bragin 22 **Under Nixon 3 million tons of bombs dropped on Indochina** 1972
USA

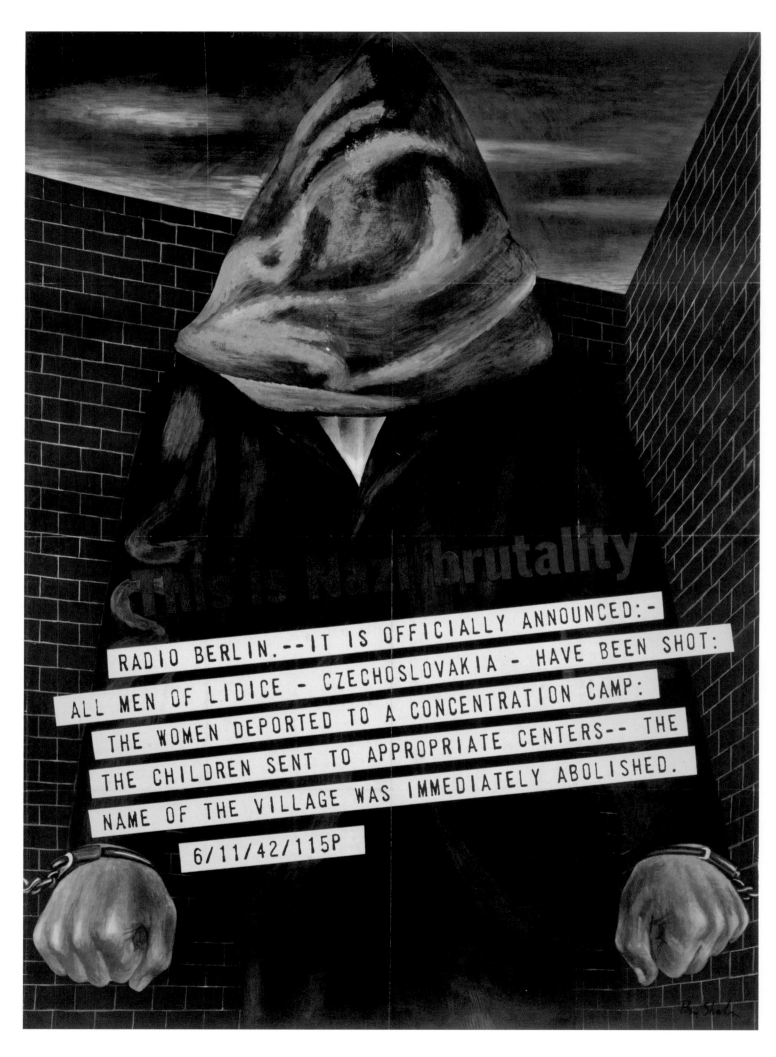

26 Ben Shahn **23** **This is Nazi brutality** 1942
USA

Stop the War Coalition

END THE TORTURE

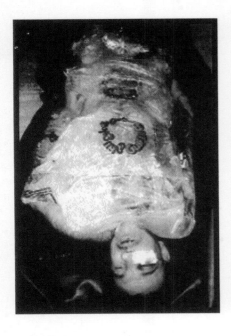

BRING THE TROOPS HOME NOW

020 7053 2153/4/5/6   www.stopwar.org.uk

Printed by East End Offset Ltd (TU), London E3. ☎ 020 7538 2521

THE POSTER. PROPAGANDA AND PUBLICITY

23 Page 26
The poster commemorates the massacre
in 1942 by the Nazis of the citizens of
the village of Lidice in Czechoslovakia
in reprisal for the assassination in Prague
of Reinhard Heydrich, Deputy Reich
Protector of Bohemia and Moravia

26 Above right
This is one of a series of nationalist
posters by David Wilson that illustrates
the mocking of noncombatant British
fishermen at the hands of the Germans,
following their capture in the North Sea.

27 Opposite
The graves of 5,000 Polish officers were
discovered in 1943 and the Allies, anxious
not to offend the Soviets, held the Nazis
responsible. Only in 1990 did Soviet
President Mikhail Gorbachev officially
admit to the Kremlin's responsibility for
the massacre.

PROPAGANDA STORIES

28   Fernando C. Amorsolo **25 Your liberty bond will help stop this** c.1917–18   David Wilson **26 How the Hun hates!** 1915–18
USA/Philippines   UK

Theo Matejko 27 **Katyn, paradise below ground** 1943
Germany

28 Below

The United States Holocaust Memorial Museum is dedicated to the victims of the Holocaust in particular, and to victims of tyranny in general. Its Committee on Conscience has focused on atrocities committed in Darfur since 2004.

29 Opposite

This anti-war poster makes propaganda from the massacre of civilians in My Lai by American troops during the Vietnam War. The photograph was published in *Life* **magazine in December 1969, almost two years after the event.**

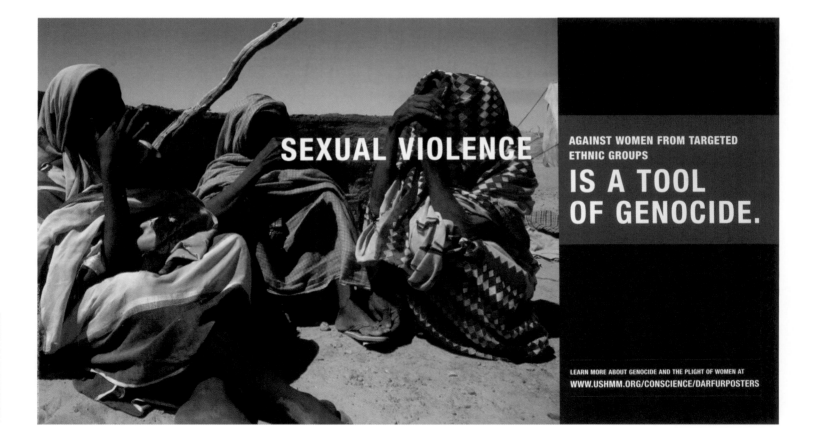

SEXUAL VIOLENCE

AGAINST WOMEN FROM TARGETED ETHNIC GROUPS

IS A TOOL OF GENOCIDE.

LEARN MORE ABOUT GENOCIDE AND THE PLIGHT OF WOMEN AT
WWW.USHMM.ORG/CONSCIENCE/DARFURPOSTERS

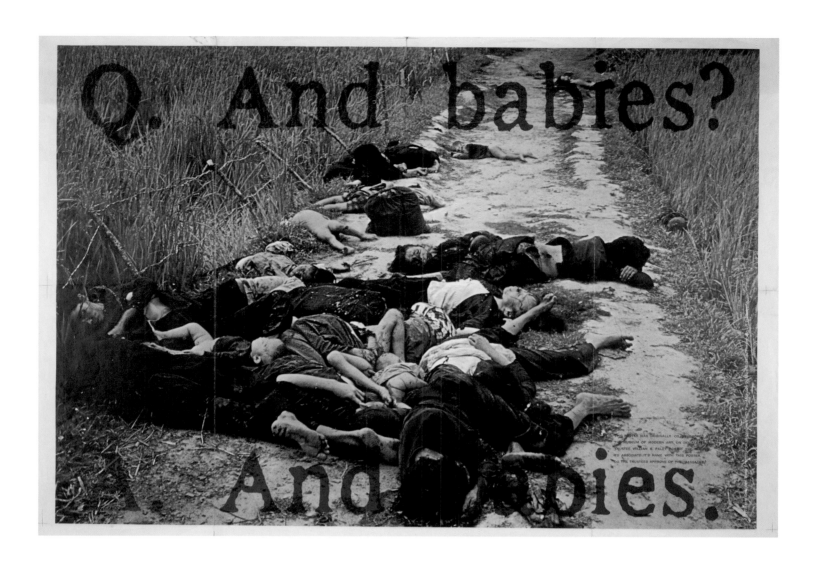

Fraser Dougherty, Jon Hendricks and Irving 29 **Q. And babies? A. And babies** 1969
Petlin (photograph by Ronald Haeberle)   USA

Les femmes et les enfants d'Europe accusent!

Par la R.A.F.

C'est l'Angleterre qui a jeté les premières bombes le 12 janvier 1940 sur la population civile

Theo Matejko 30 **The women and children of Europe accuse!** 1940
Germany

This German poster was created for occupied France and highlights the devastating effects of the bombing of French towns by the RAF during the Second World War. However, it is useful to note that the wrong date for the first RAF bombing of civilians appears on this poster, suggesting a slip by Nazi propagandists. It was on 12 May 1940, not January, that the RAF made their first raid on the German town of Mönchengladbach (when four civilians were killed, including an Englishwoman living there). Nazi propaganda made much of this, but the people responsible for the production of this poster mixed up the date. One can only presume that Goebbels (Nazi Minister for Public Enlightenment and Propaganda) was unimpressed.

Recording the Republican reaction to the bombing of the northern Spanish town of Guernica by the German Luftwaffe in support of General Franco during the Spanish Civil War, this poster was published in Spanish, English and French so as to gain international support for the Republican cause.

Attributed to Augusto **31 What are you doing to prevent this?** 1937
(photograph by Robert Capa) Spain

Viktor Koretsky **32 Red Army soldier, save us!** 1943
USSR

David Tartakover **33** **Stop the killing of children** 1991
Israel

Kein Blut für Öl!

Hände weg vom Irak!

Dieses Plakat wird unterstützt durch:

Internationale Frauenliga für Frieden und Freiheit (ISFF) ● Deutscher Friedensrat ● Friedensglockengesellschaft Berlin e. V. ● Attac Jugend Berlin ● Attac Frauennetz ● WOF! Plannungsgemeinschaft ● Demokratische Linke

www.kein-blut-fuer-oel.net

Unknown 34 **No blood for oil! Hands off Iraq!** 2003
Germany

35

35 Opposite
Joseph Stalin gave a portfolio of anti-Fascist
designs to Lord Beaverbrook when visiting
Moscow in his capacity of Minister of
Supply in 1941. These were reproduced in
English-language versions and distributed
by the Ministry of Information for exhibition
as part of a pro-Russian campaign. In 1942
they were also published in book form under
the title *The Spirit of the Soviet Union*.

36 Above left
Designed for the Artist for Victory
competition held at the Museum of
Modern Art (MoMA), New York, in 1942. It
won first prize in the 'Nature of the Enemy'
section.

37 Above right
This poster was one of six designs Lindsay
created for the last recruiting campaign
by the Government of Australia during the
First World War. It was followed at intervals
by 'Be Quick', 'God Bless Daddy', 'Will you
Fight?', 'The Last Call' and 'Fall in'. The
Armistice was signed before the
last two were issued.

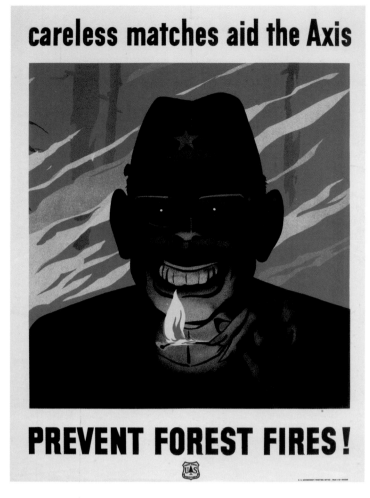

Rieuiey **38** **German women's protest against the coloured occupation troops on the Rhine** 1923–24
Germany

Unknown **39** **Prevent forest fires! Careless matches aid the Axis** 1942
USA

AIXAFEM EL FEIXISME

Editat per la Comissaria de Propaganda de la Generalitat de Catalunya.   (Fot. Català)

Pere Català Pic (Roca) **41** **Smash Fascism** 1936
Spain

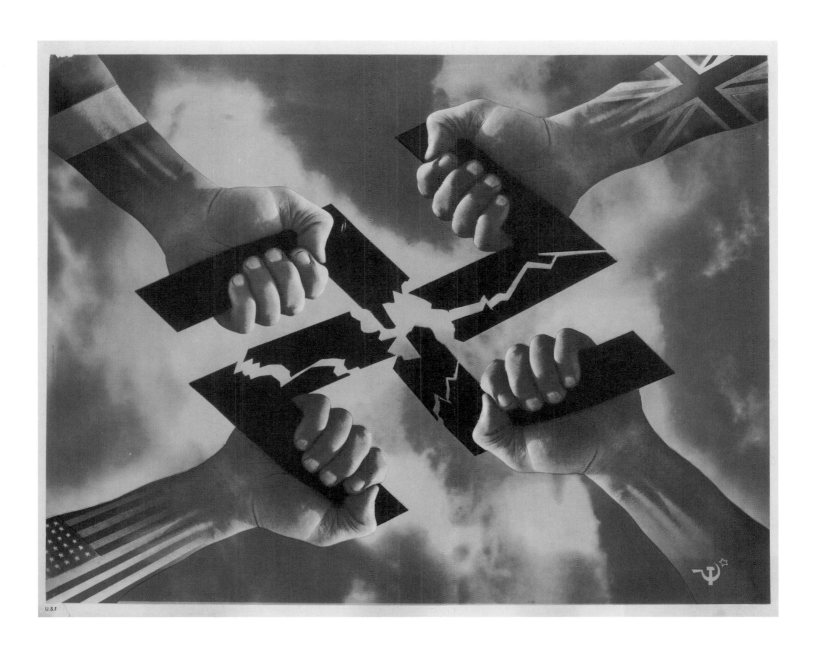

F. H. K. Henrion 42 **Untitled** 1944
USA

Otto Lehmann 43 **Help our men in uniform break England's power** 1917
Germany

Guy Lipscombe **44** **It's our flag. Fight for it. Work for it** 1915
UK

43

THE POSTER, PROPAGANDA AND PUBLICITY

2

The First World War: Selling the War and the Peace

WAR AND ADVERTISING

In Western liberal democracies the relationship between propaganda, public information and advertising is intimate. During the First World War, war imagery infiltrated the illustrated press, cartoons, the popular print, film, theatre and the music hall. It also played a part in advertising for a wide range of goods from Burberry greatcoats to Sunlight soap, and from Player's or Capstan Navy Cut tobacco to OXO cubes. The resulting imagery was strident and heroic, or domesticated and humorous, rather than sombre and reflective, or in any way realistic. A vivid illustration of the ways in which popular imagery relied upon structures of meaning embedded in various media (such as cartoons and the theatre) is the poster for 'The Johnson 'Ole' or 'Bairnsfatherland', as performed at the London Hippodrome in 1916 (69).

We can explore the mechanisms whereby the war sold products and products sold the war by looking at Bert Thomas' ''Arf a 'mo' Kaiser!' (63), which was used in a marketing campaign to raise funds to buy tobacco for servicemen. After it appeared on posters, display cards and shop windows, this poster boosted both sales of tobacco and the patriotic credentials of the *Weekly Dispatch*, and its success stimulated discussion in the media, parliament, the pulpit and the public house. *The Billposter* reported it in February 1915 as being the funniest picture of the war, and according to an American journalist its humour was seen as one of the best reasons for backing the Allies.

Just as advertisements for soap promoted modern labour-saving efficiency in order to increase leisure time (so as to make people all the fresher for the fight), so ''Arf a 'mo' Kaiser!' sold

45 Opposite
A girl from the Norfolk town of Thetford, at work with ladder and paste, carries on her father's appointment of Official Bill Poster and Town Crier, during the First World War.

A. Grebel 46 **Hey lads!** 1915
France

a recognizable image of the people to the people. Here the good-humoured self-reliant British Tommy showed what life *wasn't* like at the front, and satisfied the wish of the troops to conceal the truth for fear of upsetting those at home. OXO also made use of cheery letters from the front to emphasize qualities of strength and fitness, with posters depicting nothing more dangerous than, for example, a sun-drenched bivouac (64). These pictures of good-humoured stoicism were commonplace, and advertisements for products as diverse as sparkling wine in France (46) and bicycle tyres in Britain (65) appeared to boost morale successfully.

The marketing of products in Imperial Germany tended to be more 'dignified'. A poster for Bulgarian Hero cigarettes (62) included a melodramatic image of a soldier whose grim determination contrasts with the cocky defiance of the freeborn Englishman and the *joie de vivre* of the Republican Frenchman. Mihály Biró's romantic and dramatic realization for one of the first orchestrated advertising campaigns in Austria-Hungary emphasizes higher cause rather than humorous resignation (47). Likewise, the poster for the tonic Biocitin (66) has nothing of the levity of Bert Thomas' poster for "'Fag' Day' (121).

The imagery of war in advertising posters was often extended to political figures. Statesman Georges Clémenceau (whose nickname was 'the Tiger') was depicted in a French poster as a tiger holding up a packet of breakfast cereal to the French parliament with the words 'Energy, health and strength' written across it, cleverly linking the supposed benefits of the cereal and his own energetic leadership in pursuit of the war (67).

Meanwhile technological optimism permeated the imaginary realm of commercial culture. A poster for the magazine *L'Heure* (70) advertised the science fantasy serial 'The machine to end the war' and was perhaps inspired by the arrival of the tank on the front in 1916. Equally powerful, but less fanciful, were the Central Powers' representations of the U-boat war. Promoted in film as the ultimate war-winning strategy (72), such technological motifs lent themselves to the simplified style of Berlin-based poster designers such as Hans Rudi Erdt (71), whose restrained and abstracted realism offered a dignified depiction of men at war.

SELLING THE WAR BY DESIGN

Outdoor advertising was closely controlled in Germany and Austria-Hungary, where it was widely regarded as vulgar and inappropriate for civic space. Commerce was associated with economic gain and moral improbity, while trade and advertising were held up as necessary evils. In this environment, the applied arts configured themselves as the moral guardians of a rapidly expanding marketplace. In other words, influential designers and

Mihály Biró **47** **Pest diary** 1917
Austria-Hungary

Jocheim 48 **The German war pan. The war memorial of the German housewife** 1917–18
Germany

Unknown 49 **Subscribe to the seventh war loan** 1917
Austria-Hungary

theorists such as the editor of the magazine *Das Plakat*, Hans Sachs, advocated good design over the techniques of the advertiser in a desire to preserve spiritual values.

In contrast to Britain and America, the sensational or overtly sentimental was to be avoided. Bernhard and the Stable artists (including Hans Lindenstaedt, Julius Klinger and Hans Rudi Erdt) worked with the Berlin printing house and advertising agency, Hollerbaum und Schmidt, to develop a specific 'poster style'. The 'object-poster' or *Sachplakat* was simple, graphic and visually arresting, and its advocates claimed it was suited to the modern urban environment where there was little time for the contemplation of elaborate allegories or descriptions (48).

The progressive poster, like the typographical poster (which made use of letters as design elements), involved an object that would appear as an integral element in the design rather than as a mere illustration. The style had been the focus of much discussion in the trade press in Central Europe, Britain and America during this period, and (as illustrated by 50, 73, 74 and 76), the use of coins in posters was a popular visual trope for designers: necessarily 'national' and conveniently engraved with its symbols.

Remote from Berlin, however, designs lay somewhere between the poster and the cartoon (50, 73–77). Julius Gipkens's poster for an exhibition of German air war trophies (78) is more effective: the silhouette of the German Imperial eagle perches on a cracked Royal Flying Corps identification roundel. Both nations are simply rendered as if they were brands.

In Germany, despite the preference of the authorities for wordy slogans and literary imagery, the object-poster survived in campaigns on the home front. They encouraged people to contribute to the war economy and to schemes aimed at alleviating shortages. These ranged from the so-called 'turnip winter' of 1916 when animal feed was diverted for human consumption and people had to gather substitutes such as acorns, beechnuts, potato peelings and vegetable leftovers, to other campaigns that encouraged the collection of women's hair, nettles for textiles, metals for war production and natural oils as petroleum substitutes (48, 79).

In 1916 the German military had handed over the official drive for war loans to experienced advertising men in what was perceived as recognition from a hostile establishment. Bernhard himself oversaw the design of all the posters and press advertisements for the campaign. As designs, they aped the form of his object-posters for commerce, although it was also thought they lacked the gripping emotionalism of Allied posters (80). And, occasionally, typographical conceits could strike an unintentionally comic note (81).

Alfred Offner **50** **Subscribe to the seventh war loan** 1917
Austria-Hungary

In Austria, the *Sezession* artists rebelled against the salon
system in the last decade of the 19th century and their
archetypal strong formal design and abstract tendencies were
easily accommodated in the pursuit of national causes such as
war loan drives (governments issued special war bonds to help
finance the war efforts by encouraging the public to buy bonds,
which could be redeemed for their original value plus interest)
(82, 83). A poster advertising the seventh war loan is typical:
paper leaflets in a combination of Imperial colours flutter down
from an aircraft to pick out a strong abstract design (49).

Contemporary German design was known in Britain but its
influence was limited, not least because of wartime anti-German
feeling, although some striking designs advertising war bonds
owed more than a little to the Berlin Poster group (84, 85).
Artfully modern designs such as these were unusual, and 'Back
the bayonets' (86) is the exception that proves the rule with its
unorthodox and capricious typography.

British, French and American designs were crude by
comparison with posters from the Central Powers. 'Eat less
bread' (87) is certainly bold, but lacks aesthetic appeal.
G. Douanne's hen (89) was one of a series designed by

Unknown **51** **You are no exception. Join now** 1914
Canada

schoolchildren that draws on the German poster style in contrast with the illustrational style of the vast majority of French war posters. An American poster combines the painterly qualities of a still life: strong graphic design and allusions to the army, offering a fortuitous comparison with the object-poster (88).

MARKETING, MASCULINITY AND COMMUNITY

'The key to the situation' is startlingly bold in its design (92). Another poster depicts a cut-out of a bare forearm and clenched fist and literally pulls no punches (91). But, for many, the vernacular of advertising was inappropriate for matters of state. Recruiting was often stimulated by references to sport, and the notice '"Springbok" continental tour' (90) makes a direct appeal to manhood and sporting prowess.

'Which ought you to wear?' (see page 2) could easily be imagined to be an advertisement for hats. It played on social roles and the status of your masculinity, as defined by your hat, placing the military life at the centre. Similarly, 'Step into your place' (94) identifies different classes and occupations by headgear, among other attributes, as a column of civilians metamorphose into marching troops.

In order to capitalize on feelings of loyalty and to exploit the war fever (that had begun to subside by the time the recruiting campaign was launched in Britain), appeals were often made to male peer groups. 'Come & join this happy throng' (93) is a good example in its depiction of a crowd of eagerly waving and smiling recruits. 'Come lad slip across and help' (95) depicts the transformation of the diffident working-class 'lad', defined by his flat cap, into the self-assured and smiling soldier. Less schematic in style is 'The Navy wants men' (96): here the men have an easy confidence and the word 'Men' in a larger point size than the rest of the caption makes the implication clear.

American recruiting posters were even more direct in their approach. Artists were well schooled in marketing techniques and posters played on notions of masculinity in different ways (97, 99, 100): an empty uniform waiting to be filled, a woman flirting and a phallic torpedo leave little to the imagination. Yet such overtly sexual references were peculiar to the American poster. Other examples adapted the language of the circus poster (98) or the rhetoric of the street in a vitriolic campaign: 'Even a dog enlists, why not you?'

Rites of passage and the blooding of boys into men are the stuff of fiction and survive to this day in the popular media. Less tenacious has been the theme of inculcating guilt for not fighting. 'You are no exception' reads the speech bubble for 'I should go BUT!!!' (51). Racked with self-doubt, the civilian in silhouette is unrealized as a man. Women and children are also

marshalled to the cause (101, 102). Auguste Leroux's poster
(104) on the other hand illustrates the French reluctance to use
American-style advertising techniques and resistance to negative
stereotyping; instead it depicts the familial fulfilment of the
fighting man. It also portrays the common soldier, or *poilu*, as
the father and protector of the nation, underlining the elevated
status of often peasant-born soldiers in French wartime society.
The same motive is portrayed in rather different visual and
textual terms in 'Oh please do! Daddy' (105). Here the aim is
seduction not affirmation. James Montgomery Flagg's
secularized allegory of the American nation as a family takes this
a step further. Uncle Sam gazes knowingly into a young boy's
eyes while offering a War Savings Certificate in one hand and a
coy-looking adolescent girl in the other (103).

ORDINARY MEN AND WOMEN

The governments of combatant nations put a great deal of effort
into trying to communicate with ordinary men and women. This
was often achieved by representing them back to themselves in
roles that were of benefit to the nation.

Two posters dealing with the relations between civilian and
military effort are particularly interesting to compare. 'We're
both needed to serve the guns!' (106), addresses working people
in an echo of socialist iconography. The state is embodied in the
figure of the common soldier as he reaches across to shake the
hand of the people, represented in the figure of the munitions
worker. A comparable poster from America (108) places analogous
figures back to back, and avoids left-wing political connotations.
Likewise, American corporations commonly published posters to
enthuse their workforce and establish their patriotic credentials,
although the practice was far less frequent in other countries
and posters that do survive are an exception (107).

Visually and textually, the war effort at home was likened to
the front in many countries. Men and women were encouraged to
be, and portrayed as, active. A Red Cross poster (52) enticed the
female viewer to join the nurses, and the English housewife was
identified with the Royal Navy at the height of the German
U-boat campaign (111). France saw herself as an agrarian society
and so posters illustrated the peasant family (110): the man at
the plough in his army helmet, and the woman with a child and
holding his rifle. Drawing on allegorical resources, this woman
became Marianne, both Liberty and the motherland in peasant
dress. This theme was repeated endlessly (109, 134, 135).

Allied soldiers are heroic, defiant and sometimes
controversially violent (112–116). Stereotypes were plentiful and
French depictions of the convivial ordinariness of the European
common soldier (117, 118) contrasted with portrayals of French

Ernest Linzell **52 Hold up your end** 1918
UK

Richard Klein **53** **Flag day** 1917
Germany

Unknown (photograph by Sampson Tchernoff) **54** **Countryless!** 1916–17
UK

colonial troops as savages (116). Yet the most widely distributed German poster of the war shows a soldier staring into space (120). His determination is echoed in a charity poster for troops at the front (119), where nothing except destiny awaits these Nietzschean heroes.

Charities operated as unofficial wings of the state. Their appeal for funds often addressed something of the reality of the war in images of the disabled. Nevertheless, stereotyped patterns repeated themselves, and the introspective, tortured and spiritual heroism of the Central Powers (53, 122) was contrasted with the good-hearted Allies (121). The displaced and the defeated were also commonplace subjects and artists worked their way through the gamut of 'realisms', from social to the photographic, in order to seduce their audiences into identifying with these victims of war (54, 123, 124).

SELLING THE NATION

The First World War committed many nations to total war. The scale of operations demanded economic, industrial and human obligation to the state on an unprecedented scale. Governments had to sell themselves to the people using visions of their nations constructed through propaganda. Nationhood only becomes national where there is an adequate system of modern communication, and to that end the task was given to publicists, designers and artists in advertising trades at different levels of development and with different ideological agendas.

The liberal democracies were pitched in a battle of rhetoric with the Central Powers, who emphasized their superior spiritual, military and historical Imperial values. The French capitalized on their Republican heritage and, with Britain, made light of Imperial legacies, while in the propaganda war Britain's reliance until 1916 on a volunteer army was crucial to the 'crusade for freedom'.

1. BRITAIN AND EMPIRE

The British government in the guise of the Parliamentary Recruiting Committee (PRC) had little or no experience of publicity, and under the stewardship of Hedley Le Bas of the Caxton Agency, responsibility was delegated to agencies and printing houses to devise the campaigns. By the time conscription had ended voluntary enlistment in 1916, the PRC had produced 12.5 million copies of 164 designs, although half of these were typographical. Five of the thirty-six printing companies involved carried out half the work, and of these David Allen and Sons printed the largest share of 1.5 million copies of forty different poster designs.

The government also used posters to get its message across through various war savings campaigns, and drew on many of the same people involved with the local recruiting committees of 1914–15 who now became representatives for the National War Savings Committee. Using local government and political party structures, associations distributed posters and organized talks, events and parades on an *ad hoc* basis. These were augmented by centrally organized events such as Tank Week and Feed the Guns Week. Most of the posters were single sheets and could easily be displayed in a variety of sites.

The agencies concentrated their sights on the aspirations of ordinary people and their sense of solidarity and community. The grand narratives of British Imperial history were largely ignored in favour of images of recruits (as the nation's physical representative) and savers, who both profited from, and became financial stakeholders in, the British war effort. Traditional symbols of nation in these posters (125, 126) were as rare as historical figures (127), and Imperial emblems had even less currency, especially after democratic emblems emerged, such as the 'busy' beaver in Canada (130). Generic figures representing labour predictably came to the fore, and with the return to civilian life at the end of the war the visual rhetoric of commerce and advertising dominated (128). Few posters dwelt on the human cost of the war, although the issue was addressed in elegiac terms in some examples from the Dominions (129).

2. FRANCE

French posters are remarkably consistent in their lithographic realism and allegorical symbolism. Soon after the 1914 German invasion, the government of the Third Republic successfully intervened in industrial relations. Symbols of the Republic and its ideals of *liberté, égalité et fraternité* proliferated. War loan schemes and charitable causes were promoted in posters through this stable vision of the nation in order to challenge the Imperial militarism of the Central Powers (131). Alongside the image of the ordinary soldier, the nation was pictured as Marianne, the emblem of Liberty and the French Republic, an allegorical figure and an ordinary woman (134). In the immediate aftermath of the war she became a symbol of peace and rebirth (135) that sat comfortably alongside images of reconstruction (133) and of melancholy expressed at the human cost of the war (132).

The design of French war posters owed little to advertising, although some artists (132) were influenced by various American examples. Advertising agents were space brokers, and did not supply copy, carry out market research, or organize campaigns. Instead, academically trained professional artists were employed directly by banks, charities or government agencies or through established lithographic studios and printing houses such as Maurice Neumont Studios and the printer Devambez.

55 Top
Recruitment posters in York Railway Station, 1915, England.

56 Above
A photograph of National War Bonds and Corps Cinema advertisements in Hinges, France, 1918.

S.E.M. (Georges Goursat) 57 **For victory subscribe to the national loan** 1916
France

R. H. Porteous 58 **Women! Help America's sons win the war. Buy US Government bonds 2nd liberty loan** 1917
USA

The content of posters came under the jurisdiction of the French Press Commission, while the government and local authorities had control over hoardings and the Morris columns (the cylindrical outdoor pavement structures typically used for displaying advertisements in Paris). Opportunities for poster dissemination were frequent: flag days were promoted by the authorities across the calendar, including many officially organized special events such as French Soldiers' Day, Serbian Soldiers' Day, Orphans' Day and War Victims' Day. Many posters were distributed in schools and children were expected to take the message home to encourage donations for war loans. The French (and German) authorities gauged public morale in relation to the progress of the war through the relative success or failure of these war loans campaigns.

3. UNITED STATES OF AMERICA

George Creel's Committee on Public Information orchestrated the US campaign. In April 1917 the Society of Illustrators, under the direction of Charles Dana Gibson, met in New York and established the Division of Pictorial Publicity to work with the Division of Advertising in order to conceive publicity campaigns. Despite President Woodrow Wilson's enthusiasm for the benefits of publicity and advertising, the government took some convincing of the value of poster campaigns. Eventually, over 700 designs were produced to encourage recruitment and to promote the Food Commission, the Red Cross, American Ambulances, American Relief and Liberty Loans. These designs were as insistent and as widely distributed as any advertising campaign. American designs tended to be more commercial but less radical than those found in either Britain or Germany: design was always less important than the ability to sell.

American billposting agencies and artists gave of their space and talents freely. A giant publicity machine haunted the nation and gave heart to the advertising industry. The presidents of the Poster Advertising Association and the Associated Advertising Club of the World urged the art, design and advertising communities to contribute to the war effort. For the evangelists of the profession, the conjunction of art and communication would educate the American public in good design and encourage them to become discriminating citizens and consumers.

Before the war, outdoor advertising had been under attack from middle-class crusaders against the evils of commercial culture. The Municipal Art Society and the National Highways Association fought hard to defend civic buildings and roadside sites from despoliation. But civic structures such as the Subtreasury building in Washington and the New York Public Library were mobilized in what was known as 'the battle of the fences' and transformed into giant billboards for the Liberty Loan and other campaigns. This transformation was a measure of the momentum built up by the wartime campaigns. The third liberty loan in April 1918 saw 9 million posters produced and some were distributed as far away as Hawaii, Alaska, Puerto Rico, Cuba, the Philippines and the US Army camps in France. For the fourth liberty loan in September 1918, 10 million posters were printed, of which 50,000 were twenty-four-sheet (that is, four sheets high by six sheets wide). The scale of the operation was huge, and what was now being marketed was the abstract idea of patriotism rather than a material product.

The US was an immigrant country and notions of the nation were potentially unstable. The government therefore promoted national unity through labour, service and the family in slogans such as: 'Together we win' (59) and 'For home and country' (137). The war effort was articulated within a language of freedom, progress and happiness. As in France, the figure of Liberty was common and she took on a number of different incarnations, not least as the mother who is the nation (58), or as the one who picks up the sword to become Victory (140). Another favourite national symbol, then as now, was the American eagle (139).

As befits a democratic nation, the imagery was most commonly aimed at ordinary citizens, reflecting back to them their strength, thriftiness and common humanity. 'Sure! We'll finish the job!' (136) encourages the viewer to identify with the down-to-earth attitude of the labourer, who will work hard and give of his earnings. Food Administration posters made a play on the sacrifices of the troops in Europe to spur on the people at home to even greater efforts. Harvey Dunn's poster entitled 'They are giving all. Will you send them wheat?' is typical of this (138).

4. GERMANY AND AUSTRIA-HUNGARY

The position of the poster artist in Germany and Austria-Hungary was as complex as it was in the rest of Europe. Artists were often members of the conservative middle classes, who like the ruling military and land-owning elites, disapproved of the excess and materialism of commercial popular culture. Instead, they promoted good design and displayed a tendency towards avant garde modernist styles that the establishment found as hard as the marketplace to accommodate.

Nevertheless, the 'democratic' medium and the advertising trade were mobilized. They favoured imagery deeply rooted in medievalist and romantic legends of race and nation – an iconography where, for example, the eagle would always fly over the dove (143). The symbolism prioritized ideas of an organic and spiritual community over a materialist and democratic society in a discourse where Germanic *Kultur* was always

James Montgomery Flagg 59 **Together we win** 1918
USA

superior to Latinate civilization. Even Lucien Bernhard, who developed the object-poster, produced work that conformed to this archaic stereotype, complementing woodcut effects with gothic script in order to dissociate this new German identity from Classical traditions. Other graphic artists were less constrained, adopting modern expressionistic, *Sezession* and symbolist styles in their work (141, 142, 144) in order to emulate high art in an imagery that was closer to poetry than to the art of selling.

The symbolism of iron is iconic of both German *Kultur* and modern industrialism and it perfectly captured the idealism and materialism of the German ideology. The sword and the forge are persistent symbols, signifying a mythic medieval Teutonic past and the power of an industrial present based on steel manufacture. The symbolism of iron echoed down the ages from the nails of the cross to medieval chivalry and crusading knighthood, and is closely related to pan-Germanic mythologies and Wagnerian visions of Siegfried and Brunnhilde's 'Light-bringing love, and laughing death' (60). Nostalgic, idealized and even quasi-mystical depictions of German peasant-life seemed to represent an organic community populated with heroes prepared to sacrifice themselves for blood and soil. These myths of a modernizing, but profoundly conservative, Wilhelmine Germany had limited effect. Chivalry might sustain the military and the land-owning classes and even socially aspirant industrialists but it did little for an increasingly politicized wider population (147, 148).

Ironically, historical references intended to promote the war effort to the citizens of Austria-Hungary instead played a part in the struggle for independence from German Imperial influence by sounding a nationalist note. Many posters harked back to the legacy of the Habsburgs (147). In Vienna, artists Otto Dix, Heinrich Lefler and others adapted the contemporary *Sezession* style in order to glorify both Empire and sacrifice using grandiose eternal flames, Imperial eagles and figures of Victory, for example (145, 146). Others were more decorative and utilized indigenous folk traditions to symbolize the linguistically defined nations that were to emerge in the aftermath of the First World War (149).

SEE THE WORLD

The end of the war signalled the rebirth of France and Belgium and the physical reconstruction of swathes of their countryside. With the return to civilian life in Britain, posters depicted a population on the road to full political enfranchisement, and in America the poster prided itself as the democratic medium *par excellence* (136).

Walter Ditz 60 **Flag day. Burn sacred flame burn. Burn and never cease to burn for the Fatherland** 1918 Germany

Even before hostilities had ceased people visited the battlefields as tourists, and with the Armistice it became a popular activity. Half the men killed in battle had no known grave, and to see where they had died played an important role in the grieving process. Reflecting this state of affairs, a railway poster (153) depicts a young woman stepping into the foreground of a battlefield. A soldier gestures towards a distance bathed in the warm glow of a spiritual realm the woman can see but never physically touch. It is a reality forever out of reach. Another (152) is similarly wistful and melancholic.

From a design point of view, some British posters aspired to the simplicity of the Berlin Poster school but rejected its conceptual sophistication in favour of a more traditional illustrative approach (61). Post-war recruiting campaigns brought us slogans such as 'See the world' (150, 151) that survived until the final break up of Empire and British military withdrawal from Asia and the Far and Middle East at the end of the 1960s, but they also brought back the spectres of misrepresentation and hyperbole that had undermined the advertising business and the poster trade since the 1890s. By 1919 many people knew that life in the services was not one long holiday and veterans defaced many of these recruiting posters.

In the former German and Austro-Hungarian Empires there was no easy return to normality. Germany's eastern borders were threatened by incursions from the newly created Polish state and there was soon widespread fear of Bolshevist uprisings. Defeat brought with it a renewed nationalism that thrived on chauvinism and a strain of anti-Semitism born of the deeply held prejudices against the commercial classes. Defeat had created a power vacuum and various paramilitary groups such as the *Freikorps* used posters to recruit for their deployment against the Communists. The resulting imagery ranged from the traditionally heroic (156) to techniques learned from the British. Specifically 'Your country needs you!' addressed the viewer directly rather than through some abstract ideal of heroism (155). In one recruiting poster designed by Ludwig Hohlwein for the Steel Helmet Cadets (later incorporated into the Nazi Youth), a figure even casts a wry smile towards the observer to beguile rather than confront (154).

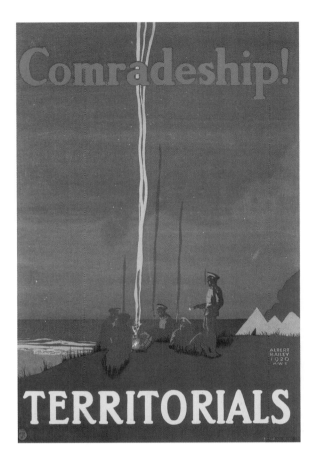

Ludwig Hohlwein 62 **Bulgarian Hero cigarettes** 1914–18
Germany

Bert Thomas **63** '**Arf a 'mo' Kaiser!** 1914
UK

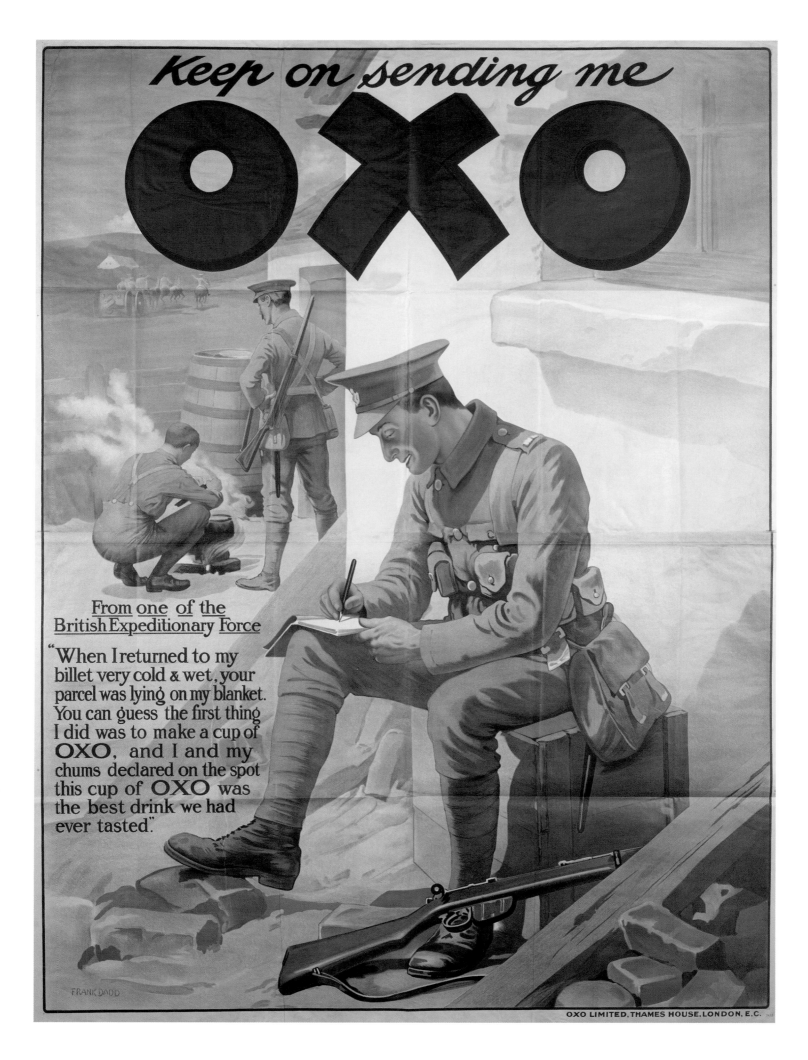

Frank Dadd **64 Keep on sending me OXO** 1914
UK

67 Opposite

This poster depicts Georges Clémenceau who was French Premier in the later stages of the First World War. He was nicknamed 'the Tiger' because of his aggressive prosecution of the war against Germany. At home he crushed anti-war dissent and even accused his pacifist Interior Minister, Louis Malvy, of treason.

68 Page 64

Cabaret and music halls were important diversions for the troops. Posters advertising popular entertainments in France retained the lightness of touch characteristic of French poster design from the 1880s, and especially drawn from the work of artists Chéret and Toulouse-Lautrec.

69 Page 65

Originally published in *The Bystander* magazine, Bruce Bairnsfather's cartoon character 'Old Bill' found its way onto posters through a stage adaptation performed at the London Hippodrome in 1916. A 'Jack Johnson' was a nickname for a German shell.

Georges Dola **68** **Film concert for the Allies** 1918
France

Henri Montassier **70** **L'Heure has discovered the machine to end the war** 1917
France

70 Opposite

This poster acknowledged the scale of destruction that resulted from modern industrialized conflict, and offered hope for victory through new technology. Montassier's machine makes no reference to contemporary tanks and has, for example, more in common with the science fiction machines used by the invading Martians in H. G. Wells' *The War of the Worlds*, 1898.

71 Above left

Early in 1917, generous military sponsorship and an effective pictorial propaganda bureau transformed Germany's propaganda output. The Königliche Bild und Film-Amt (Bufa) aimed to promote military successes to a war-weary German public and also to neutral countries. Hans Rudi Erdt's economic design using areas of flat colour, hand-drawn lettering and semi-abstract shapes is characteristic of German graphics of this period.

72 Above right

This Hungarian poster advertises the German propaganda film, *U-Boote Heraus!* (The U-Boats are out!). Hans Rudi Erdt designed the German version for the same film. 'Urania' is the name of the cinema showing the film.

Hans Rudi Erdt 71 **With our boys in blue** 1917
Germany

S. L. Satori 72 **The U-Boats are out!** 1917
Hungary

L'Or Combat Pour La Victoire

Jules Abel Faivre **73** **Pour forth your gold for France** 1915
France

T. Martin Jones 75 **Buy war loan bonds** 1918
India

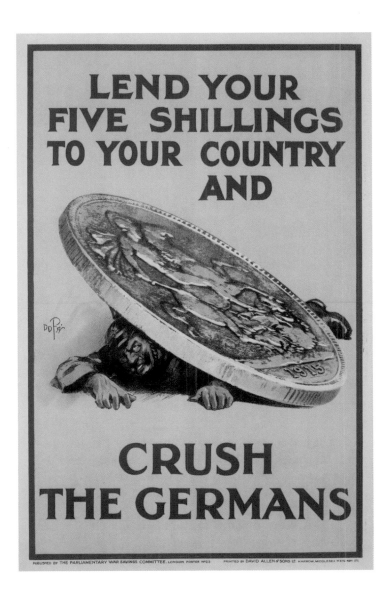

73 Page 68

The cockerel, known as the 'Coq Gaulois' is the national symbol of France and is derived from the Latin word *gallus*, which means both 'Gaul' and 'rooster'. Since 1848, the Gallic rooster has appeared on the official seal of the French Republic.

74 Page 69

The image of a coin used as a shield in this poster conveyed the message that the money raised by war loans would help to defend the nation. Other poster designers used similar images, including Mihály Biró and Alfred Offner.

76 Above left

The British crown, which is both a coin (portrayed here as a five shilling piece) and government, literally and metaphorically crushes the Kaiser in this poster.

77 Above right

A faux montage technique is used in this poster to give the illusion of money being turned into ammunition.

79 Page 73

In this poster, 'train oil' (or *tran*) is a generic term used to describe oils derived from marine animals. Oils such as these would have been used as fuel.

D. D. P. **76** **Lend your five shillings to your country and crush the Germans** 1915
UK

Unknown **77** **Turn your silver into bullets at the Post Office** 1915
UK

Julius Gipkens **78 DELKA – German Air-War Trophies Exhibition** 1917
Germany

Julius Gipkens **79** **Fishermen, bring train oil! Catch porpoises and seals!** 1917–18
Germany

Lucien Bernhard 80 **Eighth war loan** 1918
Germany

Euringer 81 **Citizens of Cologne. Sixth war loan** 1917
Germany

Julius Klinger 82 **Eighth war loan** 1918
Austria-Hungary

Emil Ranzenhofer 83 **Subscribe to the eighth war loan** 1918
Austria

86 | Opposite

This poster was based on Nevinson's poster design to promote his second exhibition at the Leicester Galleries in March 1918. On 21 July 1918 Nevinson wrote to the social reformist C. F. G. Masterman at the War Propaganda Bureau: 'Could you advise me as to whom to apply to on the War Bond Poster Dept as I want to give them my red bayonet poster. They seem to want it as I notice they are always cribbing it – and none too well – in some effect or other.'

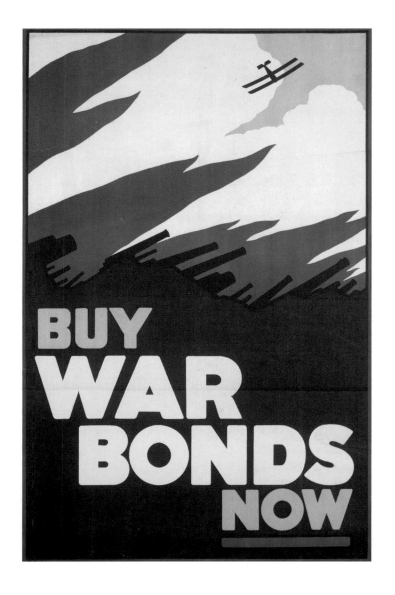

Unknown | 84 | **Buy war bonds now** 1918
UK

Unknown | 85 | **Buy your war bonds now!** 1918
UK

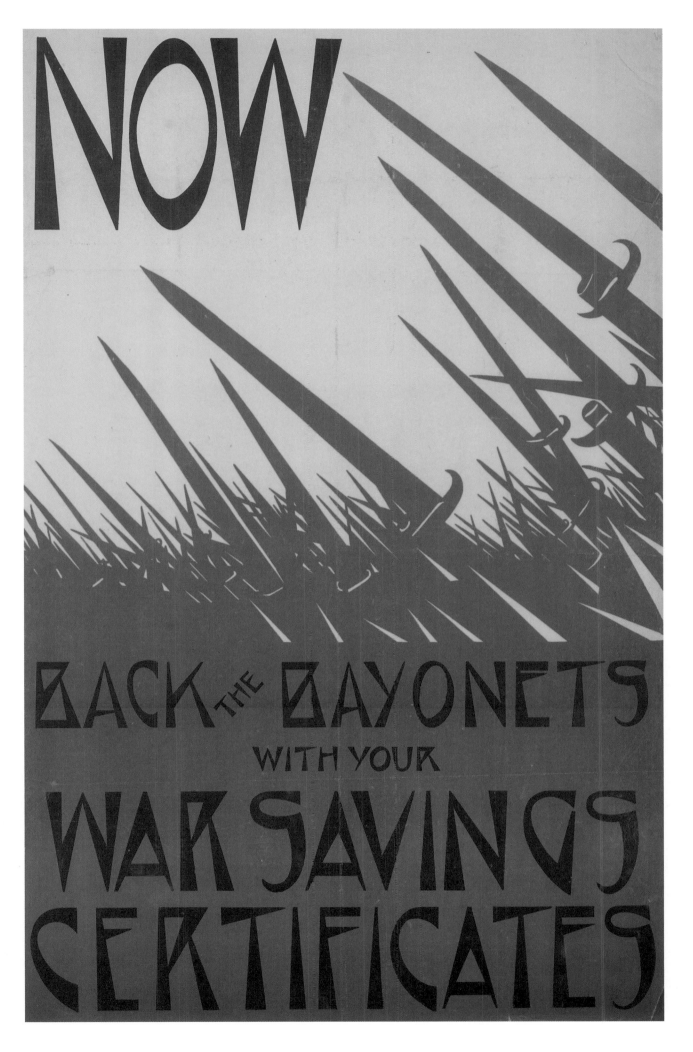

After C. R. W. Nevinson 86 **Now, back the bayonets** 1918
UK

Unknown **87** **Eat less bread** 1917
UK

This is one of a distinguished series of posters made to the same format and size designed by schoolchildren for a food conservation campaign. Douanne was aged just sixteen when she produced this exceptional design.

John E. Sheridan **88** **Food is ammunition – don't waste it** 1918
USA

G. Douanne **89** **Let's look after the farmyard** c.1916
France

"SPRINGBOK" CONTINENTAL TOUR

Via POTCHEFSTROOM, WOKING, FLANDERS, and the RHINE

FREE RETURN PASSAGES, including entire Outfit, Food, Accommodation, and Medical Attendance, may be booked at nearest Recruiting Office.

DON'T MISS THIS CHANCE TO SEE THE WORLD'S GREATEST SPECTACLE

LEND YOUR STRONG RIGHT ARM TO YOUR COUNTRY ENLIST NOW

PUBLISHED BY THE PARLIAMENTARY RECRUITING COMMITTEE LONDON. POSTER N°2

H. & C. GRAHAM LTD. LONDON S.E.

92 Opposite

Appealing to notions of adulthood, a key is used in this poster as a symbol of the rite of passage from childhood to adult status, which was legally acquired at the age of twenty-one in the UK.

80   Top: Unknown **90** **"Springbok" Continental Tour** 1918
South Africa

Above: Unknown **91** **Lend your strong right arm to your country. Enlist now** 1914
UK

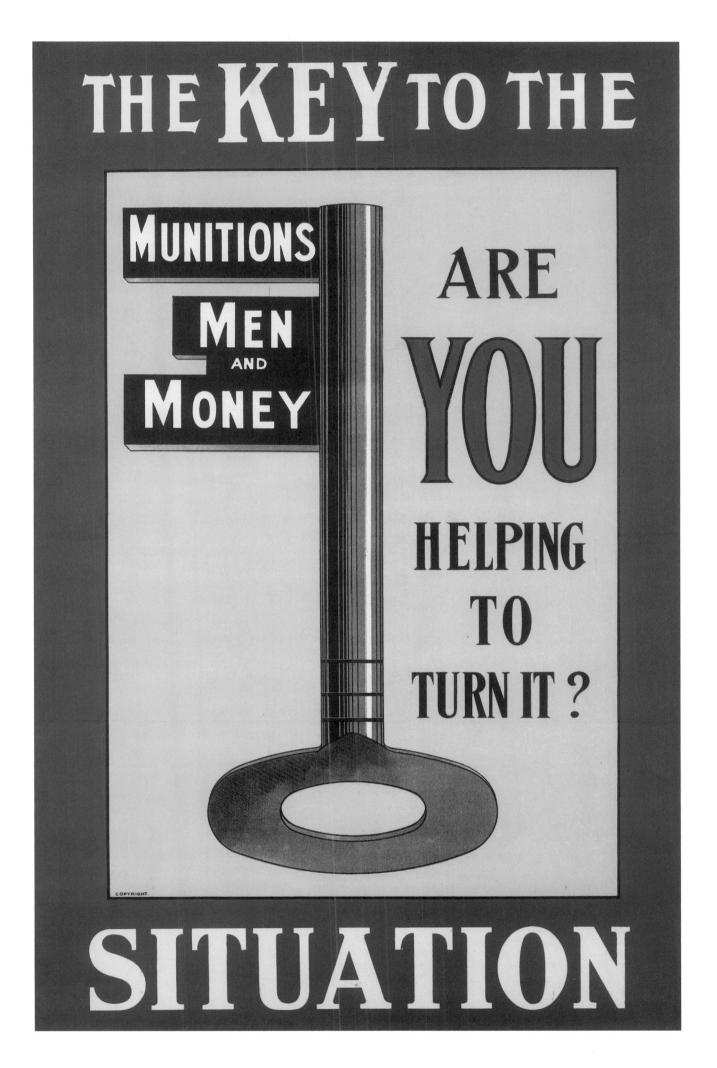

Top: Unknown 93 **Come & join this happy throng off to the front** c.1915–16
Ireland

Above: Unknown 94 **Step into your place** 1915
UK

COME LAD
SLIP ACROSS AND HELP

Unknown **96** **The Navy wants men** 1917
Canada

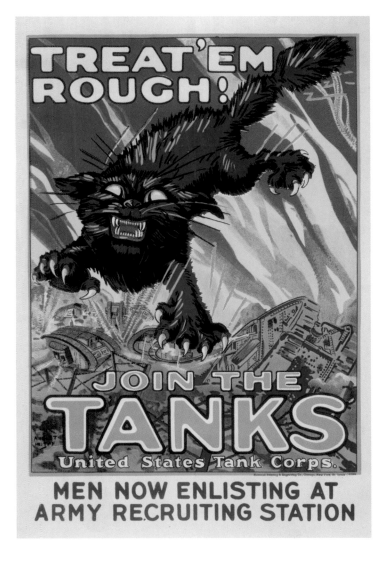

Charles Stafford Duncan 97 **It takes a man to fill it. Join the Navy** 1917
USA

August William (Angiet) Hutaf 98 **Treat 'em rough! Join the tanks** 1918
USA

Howard Chandler Christy **99** **Gee!! I wish I were a man, I'd join the Navy** 1917
USA

Richard Fayerweather Babcock 100 **Join the Navy. The service for fighting men** 1917
USA

THE FIRST WORLD WAR: SELLING THE WAR AND THE PEACE

87

Savile Lumley 101 **Daddy, what did YOU do in the Great War?** 1915
UK

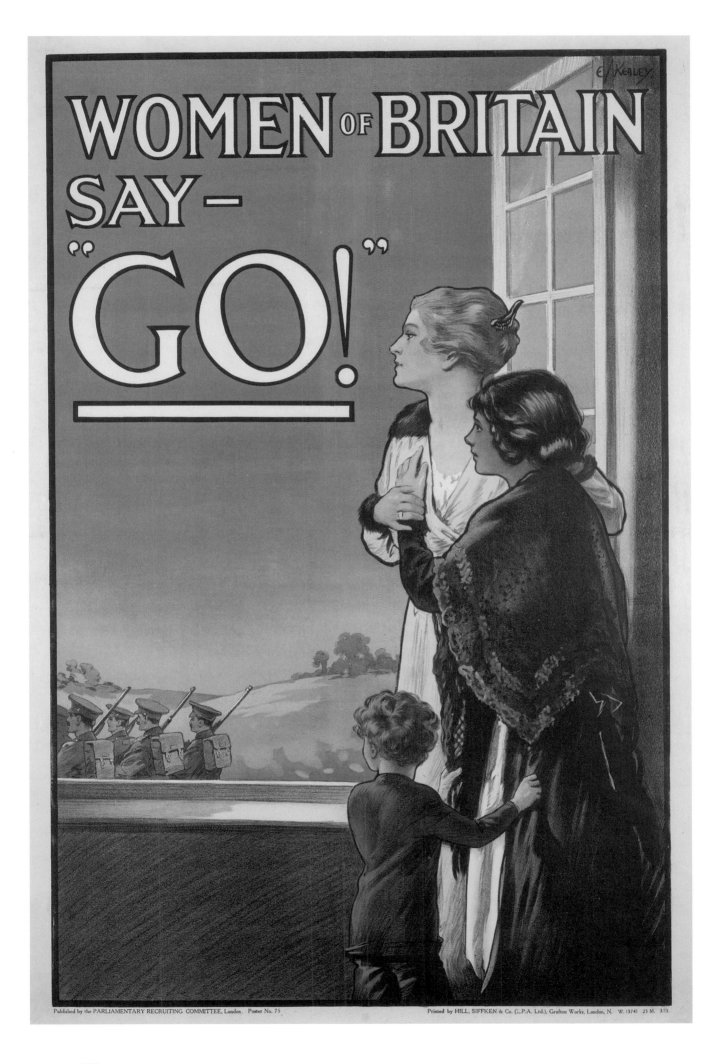

E. V. Kealey 102 **Women of Britain say – "Go!"** 1915
UK

James Montgomery Flagg **103 Boys and girls! You can help your Uncle Sam win the war** 1917
USA

Auguste Leroux [104] **Subscribe for France who fights! For the girl growing up every day** 1917
France

Joseph Earnest Sampson [105] **Oh please do! Daddy. Buy me a victory bond** 1917
Canada

Top: Unknown **106** **We're both needed to serve the guns!** 1915
UK

Above: Welsh **107** **Put the Hun on iron rations** 1914–18
UK

STAND BY THE BOYS IN THE TRENCHES
MINE MORE COAL
UNITED STATES
FUEL ADMINISTRATION

Walter Whitehead 108 **Stand by the boys in the trenches. Mine more coal** 1918
USA

109 Above

Based on a photograph by the Brown brothers, this is one of the most persistent images to emerge from the war and shows women harnessed to a plough to identify them with the land in the most literal of ways.

Unknown **109** **They are serving France. Everyone can serve** 1918
Canada

B. Chavannaz **110** **You too are doing your duty: with all your resources subscribe to the war loan** 1918
France

Unknown **111** **Don't waste bread! Save two slices every day and defeat the 'U' Boat** 1917
UK

Frank Brangwyn 112 **Put strength in the final blow. Buy war bonds** 1918
UK

112 Opposite

This poster was unique in that it managed to cause offence both in Britain and in Germany. It shocked the British National War Savings Committee who published it but found the image was too extreme to use, even in the fight against Germany. In Germany it was regarded as evidence of British barbarism and it was rumoured that the Kaiser placed a price on Brangwyn's head as a result of this poster design.

113 Above left

This is the most famous French poster of the First World War: it quotes General Philippe Pétain at the battle of Verdun, while the pose of the soldier echoes François Rude's 'Victory', on the Arc de Triomphe and invoked the principles of liberty, equality and fraternity which lay at the heart of the French Republic. Reinterpreted many times, it was later adapted by the USA during the Second World War for the 1943 poster 'We have just begun to fight!' (see page 170).

Jules Abel Faivre **113** **Let's get them!** 1916
France

Norman Alfred William Lindsay **114** **The last call** 1918
Australia

Walter Whitehead 115 **Come on! Buy more liberty bonds** 1918
USA

Charles Dominique Fouqueray 116 **African Army and Colonial Troops day** 1917
France

3e EMPRUNT
DE LA
DÉFENSE NATIONALE

J'ai une perm' vous voyez, J'viens souscrire à l'emprunt ! Faites comme moi et j'dirai qui vous avez d'la conversation

Brichou

GRAVE ET IMPRIME PAR "LA PLATINOGRAVURE"
63, Avenue de la République, MONTROUGE (Seine)

VISA 10.067

M. Kivatizky 117 **I'm on leave, you see. I'm coming to subscribe to the loan!** 1917
France

99

Théophile Alexandre Steinlen **118 Serbia day** 1916
France

Lina von Schauroth 119 **Imperial and popular charity fund for the Army and the Navy** 1917
Germany

Fritz Erler 120 **Help us win!** 1917
Germany

Bert Thomas 121 "Fag" Day 1917
UK

Ludwig Hohlwein **122 The Ludendorff appeal for the war-disabled** 1918
Germany

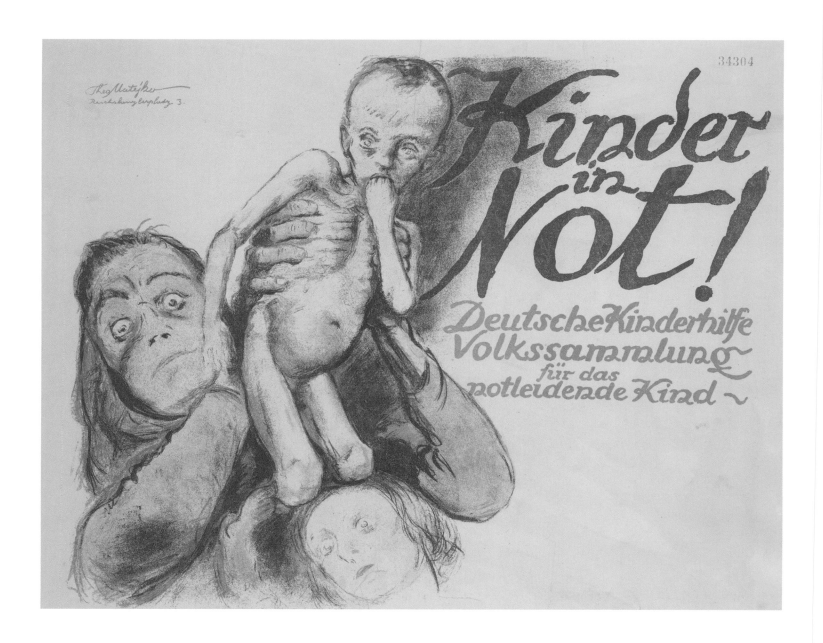

124 Opposite
This poster imposes a stereotypically 'orientalist' and decorative view onto the Near East.

Lucy Elizabeth Kemp Welch 125 **Remember Scarborough! Enlist now** 1915
UK

BRITAIN · NEEDS

YOU · AT · ONCE

PUBLISHED BY THE PARLIAMENTARY RECRUITING COMMITTEE, LONDON.   POSTER Nº 108   PRINTED BY SPOTTISWOODE & Cº LTD LONDON. E.C.

This poster uses the German First High
Seas Fleet bombardment of Scarborough
on 16 December 1914 as a rallying call
for enlistment into the British Army.

127 Below left

Joan of Arc, as an enemy of the British,
was rarely mobilized in France, but her
image as a powerful woman defiant of
the British establishment enticed women
to buy war savings certificates.

Bert Thomas **127** **Joan of Arc saved France. Women of Britain save your country.**
Buy war savings certificates 1915
UK

S. T. C. Weeks **128** **Women! Who need skilled jobs ask for free training** 1919
UK

129 Above

The poster's title is a line from the poem 'In Flanders Field' by John McRae. The poem concludes with the lines 'If ye break faith with us who die / We shall not sleep, though poppies grow / In Flanders fields'. First published in 1915, the poem is recited on Remembrance Day in Canada.

Frank Lucien Nicolet 129 "If ye break faith – we shall not sleep" 1918
Canada

Unknown 130 Keep all Canadians busy. Buy 1918 victory bonds 1918
Canada

109

Jules Abel Faivre **131 Subscribe to the fourth national loan** 1918
France

Georges Dorival **132 After hostels for soldiers, hostels for civilians** 1919
France

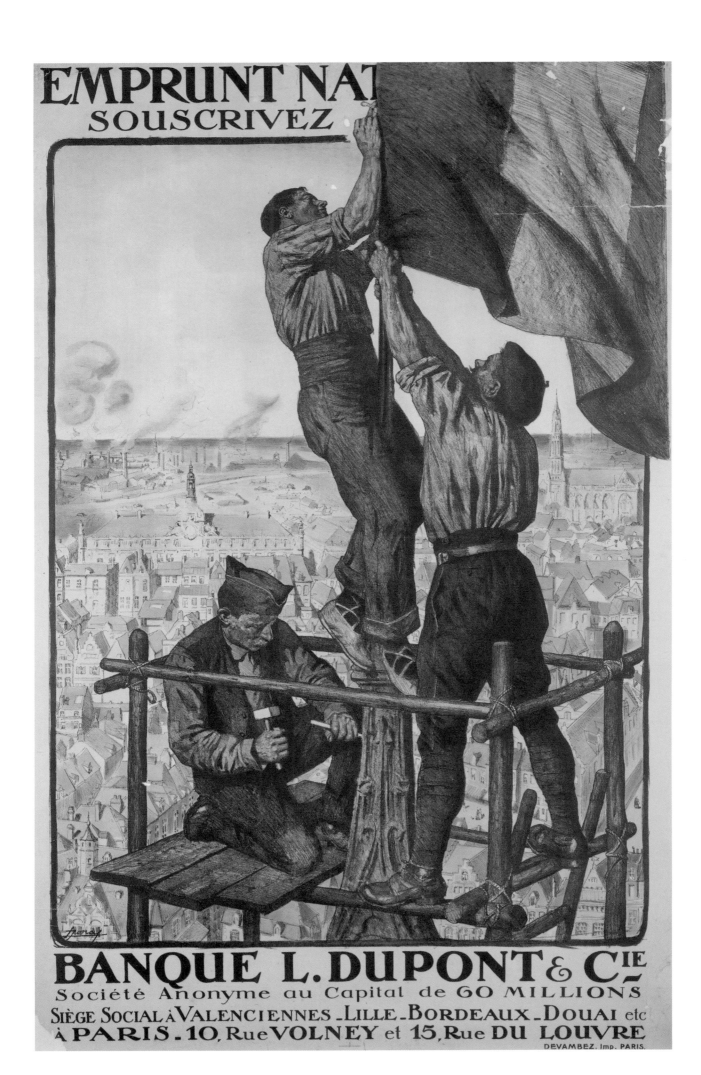

Lucien Jonas 133 **National loan, subscribe** 1919
France

Georges Scott **134 For the flag! For victory!** 1917
France

Alfonse Lelorg **135 Banque Privée. Subscribe to the reconstruction loan** 1919–20
France

Gerrit A. Beneker **136 Sure! We'll finish the job. Victory liberty loan** 1918
USA

136 Opposite
Over 3 million of these posters were distributed and in an interview with *The Poster Souvenir Edition* in 1919, Beneker said, '[I] took a working man as my hero [who was] known to every man, woman and child in the country'.

138 Above
Dunn was one of eight artists who travelled to Europe with the American Expeditionary Force. As a painter of the prairie, he transferred his sense of the wide-open spaces to the battlefield, to impose the American experience onto the European landscape.

Alfred Everitt Orr **137** **For home and country. Victory liberty loan** 1918
USA

Harvey Dunn **138** **They are giving all. Will you send them wheat?** 1918
USA

Charles Livingston Bull 139 **Join the Army Air Service. Be an American eagle!** 1917–18
USA

J. C. Leyendecker 140 **USA bonds: weapons for liberty** 1918
USA

A. W. Wurthmann **141 Those who subscribe to the seventh war loan clear the way** 1917
Germany

Paul Neumann **142 The final blow is the eighth war loan** 1918
Germany

Karl Sigrist 143 **Subscribe to the war loan** 1918
Germany

Willy Szesztokat 144 **Forge the German sword. Subscribe to the war loan** 1917
Germany

119

A. S. **145 Subscribe to the fifth Austrian war loan** 1916
Austria-Hungary

ZEICH·NET

4. KRIEGSANLEIHE

Heinrich Lefler 146 **Subscribe to the fourth war loan** 1916
Austria-Hungary

Hanuš Svoboda **147** **Subscribe to the fifth Hungarian war loan** 1916
Austria-Hungary

Erwin Püchinger 148 **Subscribe to the 5½ per cent third war loan** 1915
Austria-Hungary

Minka Podhajská 149 **Subscribe to the seventh war loan!** 1917
Austria-Hungary

Unknown 150 **Travel all over the world with the Machine Gun Corps** 1919
UK

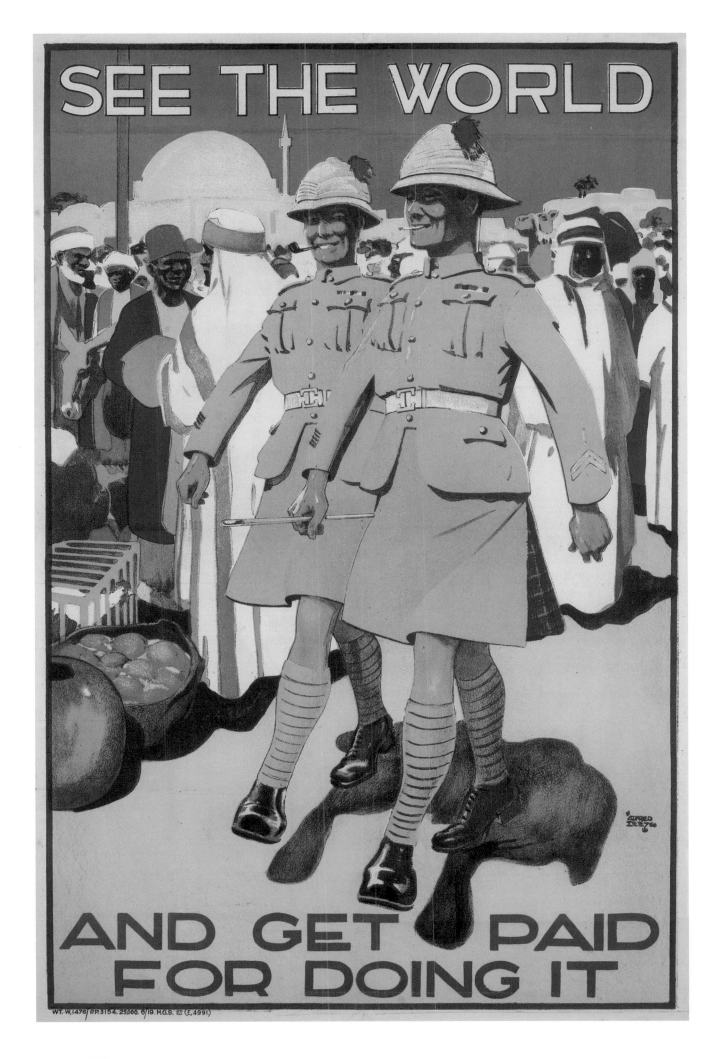

Alfred Leete **151 See the world and get paid for doing it** 1919
UK

Henri Gray 152 **Thiepval** c.1918–19
France

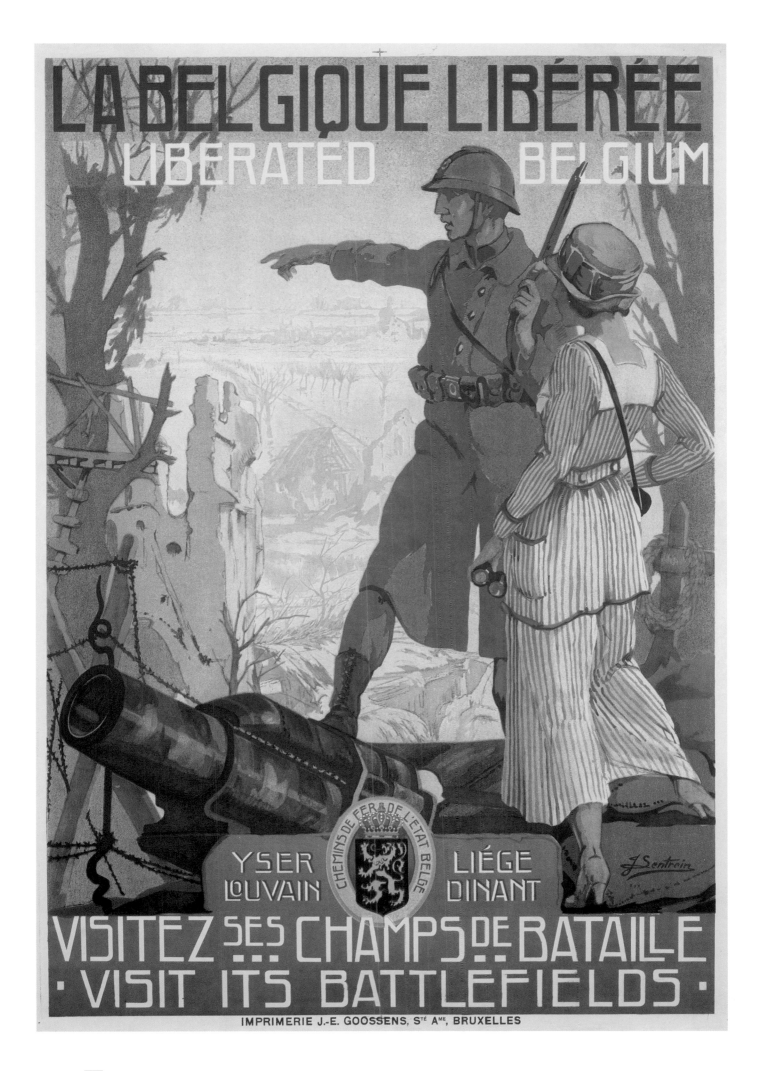

Ludwig Hohlwein 154 **Join us. Steel Helmet Cadet** 1920–23
Germany

152 Page 126

This poster was one of a series offering
rail excursions to key sites and cemeteries
along the western front following the end
of the First World War. The image refers
to the attack on the Schwaben Redoubt
at Thiepval by the 36th (Ulster) Division
on the first day of the Battle of the
Somme in 1916. The solitary infantryman
gazes towards the Connaught and Mill
Road cemeteries bearing the graves of
the fallen Ulstermen.

Julius Engelhard Ussy **155 You should join the Reich Army too** 1919
Germany

Lina von Schauroth **156 Hülsen Volunteer Corps** 1918–19
Germany

Interwar Europe:
The Ideological Battleground

After the First World War, the non-commercial poster was increasingly adapted to suit ideological and political needs. Governments had advanced their objectives during the war using propaganda for patriotic recruiting and war loans schemes. In Britain, where relatively stable political conditions prevailed, the population was represented in posters as embryonic consumers in thrall to commercial culture. But as parts of Europe descended into chaos, the traditional and conservative iconographies of the nationhood that had previously held sway held little attraction. Born from the collapse of empires, new political parties of the Left and the Right struggled to define themselves with new iconographies in the great cosmopolitan centres from Barcelona to Vienna, and Moscow to Berlin.

In the Soviet Union and Nazi Germany, democratic freedom, free enterprise and freedom of expression were overthrown by programmatic political ideologies: one based on class war and the dictatorship of the proletariat, and the other on Aryan racial superiority and military dominance. The Great Depression in the early 1930s, and concentration on heavy industry and aversion to consumerism in the Soviet Union, led to a collapse of the advertising trade. These single-party states did not tolerate dissent and tried to control artistic expression by legislation: artists found themselves confined to an anti-modernist aesthetic based on photographic realism and debased classicism.

In Spain, despite Stalin's best efforts, the Communist Party failed to subordinate the Left, and the Civil War became a struggle for the future under complex conditions. Graphic designers and artists dedicated themselves to the cause of the Republic in the name of anti-Fascism and progressive socialism, in a battle against what they saw as the dark forces of reaction and conservatism as embodied in the church, the military and the aristocracy. In this way, the trades of advertising and publishing were politicized and opened up to the kind of modernist aesthetic expression that had been previously reserved for the fine arts.

It is estimated that during the Spanish Civil War some 2,000 poster designs appeared between 1936 and 1938. Here, soldiers read posters calling women to arms in Barcelona, September 1936.

Valentin Zietara 158 **Be united!** c.1918
Germany

REVOLUTION IN GERMANY

In Germany, a diversity of styles in poster design was part of a search for meaningful modes of visual expression in an atmosphere of defeat and betrayal, which was exacerbated by civil conflict and shortages of food and fuel. As the authorities struggled to maintain order and military regulation and censorship fell away during the revolution in Berlin in November 1918, contemporaries commented on the profusion of posters in the streets.

Paul Zech, director of the Publicity Office of the Weimar Republic believed unmediated and intuitive expressionist aesthetics were immediately understandable to the general public and free of contamination from the old order and the demands of commerce. Socialist utopianism is evident in the imagery, and the use of radical imagery and aesthetics was part of a strategy to seduce hard leftists towards the more moderate position held by the Socialist Democratic government. Prevalent conditions of social anarchy produced dramatic imagery, and the consequences of strikes, for example, were framed in terms of starvation and death (167, 168).

The expressionist agenda failed – dismissed by Leftists because it denigrated the human body, and by the bourgeoisie as more suited to the expression of individual angst than political ideals. As a result, the Publicity Office shifted its focus without losing its fascination with sensationalist imagery. Death stalked the land as blood-drenched and bomb-throwing anarchy (170). The imagery drew on the 'lower' reaches of popular culture evident in cinema posters and pulp literature. A Communist poster, on the other hand, transformed the rhetoric of the *Communist Manifesto* into the visual language of the cartoon (169).

But Munich's *Sezession* and Berlin's poster style of the First World War contributed to the visual identity of regional parties. A poster in the Munich style for the German People's Party in Bavaria and the German Democratic Party (163) shows an unlikely alliance of national, conservative, Catholic and liberal parties. Another draws on the legacy of the object-poster in a design bearing the slogan 'The German Democratic Party is the party of women' (164). The modernity of the abstract pattern of the national colours failed to represent visually the new position of women. Poster designers were now faced with the new problem of addressing women in other roles than mother and nation, war worker or nurse.

REVOLUTION IN HUNGARY

Following the end of the First World War, the political situation in the newly established Hungarian Republic was as unstable as it was in Germany, and in many areas government authority simply did not exist. In Budapest, the Social Democrats allied with the Communists to form the Hungarian Socialist Party and established the Hungarian Soviet Republic. The aristocracy lost its landed estates and many of

158
German political parties followed fault lines of class, religion and region, and their rhetoric and negative campaigning exaggerated divisions in German society during the early 20th century. As early as 1917, the German Fatherland Party was founded by right-wing militarists with an imperialist and expansionist agenda. In the opposite poster, the party's call for unity was symbolized by the head of the German imperial eagle, while its romantic conservatism was expressed by the primitive style and use of gothic script.

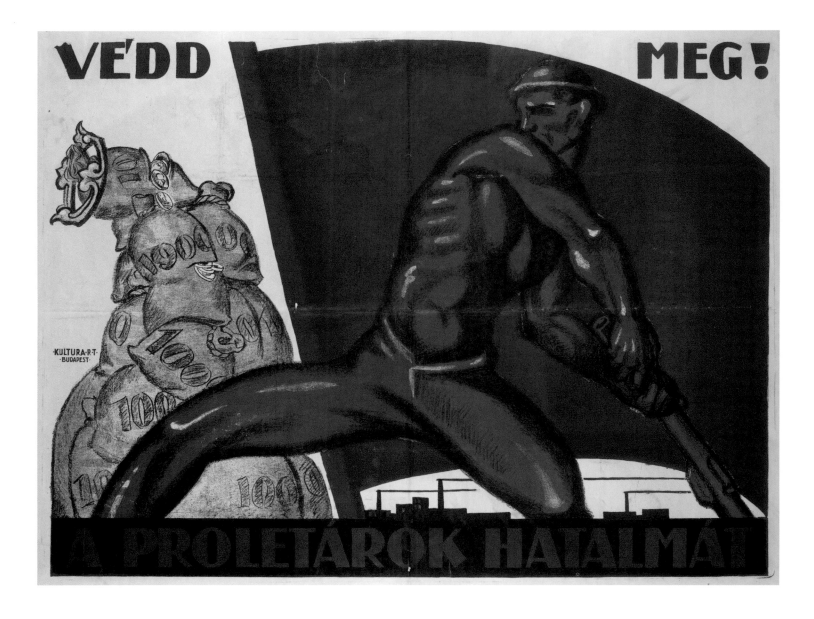

VÉDD   MEG!

A PROLETÁROK HATALMÁT

159

The Hungarian Soviet Republic produced
some fifty official designs. Artists Tabor and
Dankó were associated with the Group of
Eight who adapted secessionist and art deco
cubist styles to political ends. The stylized
figure of a worker, stereotypically naked
to the waist, attacks a pile of money bags
topped with a crown signifying capital,
aristocracy, monarchy and Empire.

its privileges, the church was separated from the state and the
people were guaranteed freedom of speech and assembly. But
increasing violence and shortages of food and fuel eventually led
to the establishment of a right-wing régime under Miklós Horthy.

Hungarian designers engaged with socialist iconographies of
the worker, oppression, exploitation and resistance. Lajos Santo,
a member of the Artists' Advertising Workshop, confronts the
observer with the march of a Christ-like proletariat, inhibited
only by a crown of thorns around their ankles, signifying their
collective sacrifice and redemptive force (174).

'They wash themselves!' adapts the same iconography of the
counter-revolution (175). The worker, bathed in red, washes his
hands in the rivers of blood flowing from the Hungarian parliament.
This bestial figure re-emerges in the right-wing anti-socialist, anti-
Semitic and anti-Communist propaganda of the time, sometimes
as a monster, often as a sexual predator, occasionally as a hyena,
stereotypically associated with blood-soaked landscapes.

RED VIENNA

Conditions were similar in Vienna and severe food and housing shortages propelled the democratically elected Social Democratic Party to power in May 1919. In 1921, challenged by the right-wing agrarian Christian Socialist Party, the Social Democrats established Vienna as an independent province to protect its socialism. A Communist Party poster referred to the housing shortages, squatter organizations and the radical architectural schemes proposed by the municipal authorities (159). The creation and manipulation of culture by the socialists in Vienna followed the pattern in Germany. Deeply suspicious of mass commercial culture that they believed had seduced the workers, they at first adopted expressionist styles before incorporating elements from socialist realism and popular culture into their posters (171).

A Christian Democratic poster made good use of cartoon symbolism to turn Communist rhetoric against itself (172). A Red worker turns the press labelled 'taxes' to squeeze the middle classes dry in a suitably bloody image. ('Taxes' in German allows a pun on the word meaning 'to steer' and refers to the Communist Party's self-description as the helmsman of society.) The Bolsheviks, and in Vienna the municipal authorities, were widely identified with the Jews, and Bernd Steiner's overtly anti-Semitic poster depicted the Jewish–Bolshevik snake strangling the eagle of the Austrian Republic (173).

THE USSR AND THE BOLSHEVIK REVOLUTION

Tsarist Russia engaged the Central Powers on the eastern front, but the war did not go well, and revolutions took place in Petrograd (now St Petersburg) and Moscow just as they later did in Berlin, Munich, Budapest and Vienna. Demonstrations and strikes in Moscow were followed by a mutiny of the Petrograd garrison and the takeover of the city in the February Revolution of 1917. Subsequent political manoeuvring led to the abdication of the Tsar and the establishment of the Russian Republic.

Petrograd resembled other major urban centres in Europe at that time, with shortages of essentials precipitating social and industrial unrest. By the summer of 1917, the Russian army, reduced by mutinies and mass desertions, was no longer prepared to fight. As conditions worsened in the cities, so the authority of Alexander Kerensky's Provisional Government weakened and the influence of the Bolsheviks increased. After the Bolshevik Revolution in October of the same year, Lenin concluded a separate peace with the Central Powers, and Civil War broke out.

The wars, revolutions and civil unrest severely disrupted the printing and publishing industry and restricted paper supplies. But the political situation made the poster a highly efficient medium of communication among a largely illiterate population.

161 Top
The view of the interior of a Russian
Communist Propaganda train in the 1920s.

162 Above
Decoration of a Russian public building
in 1926.

Russia did not have a large investing public and war loans did not play a significant part in war finance. Nevertheless, schemes were launched by the Tsarist and Provisional Governments to generate financial support for the army. Examples from 1916 aimed at the work force at home or in the military (178) were sober and avoided overt Imperial symbolism so as to appeal to the increasingly radicalized urban and industrial classes. Provisional Government posters, however, were more declamatory and politicized: designs by Butchkin (177) and Kustodiev (176) adopted the political symbolism of the soviet, the red flag and the agitator. Both address the audience directly as a potential participant rather than a sympathetic observer. These techniques belonged to the advertising trade, a point not lost on Russian artists Rodchenko and Mayakovsky, whose successful advertising agency during the 1920s was driven by their awareness of advertising's formal relationship with agitation, according to historian Christina Kiaer in her book *Imagine No Possessions: The Socialist Objects of Russian Constructivism*. Interestingly, there had been a display of British wartime art in Moscow in 1916 and Alfred Leete's legacy (see 16, page 20) can be seen in Bolshevik posters (182). What is also clear through the Provisional Government's transformation of public culture is that the symbolism and propaganda techniques of the Bolshevik Revolution were already in place.

Distinctively Bolshevik posters introduced the symbols of Communist revolution in Petrograd in late summer 1918, including the hammer and sickle, the red star, heroic workers and peasants. During the Civil War, these posters were mainly published by the Litizdat (the Bolshevik organization which was responsible for Red Army propaganda), which was presided over by Bolshevik revolutionary Leon Trotsky. A poster celebrating the first anniversary of the Red Army in 1919 contains the typical revolutionary symbols arranged in the manner of a classical emblem, complete with laurels and in a shallow relief space (181). Here socialist realism betrayed its origin in the bourgeois commercialism of the engraved banker's draft, which was at least as strong an influence as the popular culture of the cinema poster, illustration and the *lubok* (a Russian popular print). Christian, Classical and national iconographies were, it seems, adapted as and when needs required. In contrast, 'For one Russia', produced on behalf of the White Armies (who opposed the Bolsheviks and fought against the Red Army during the Civil War of 1918–21), is rooted in traditional illustration with its heroic depiction of the white St George descending onto the red dragon (180). This allegorical design drew yet further meaning: St George is the patron saint of Moscow, which is the city depicted in the background of this poster.

The imagery typical of Russian posters after the First World War often literally translates the highly charged figurative language of Communist polemicists into visual imagery. The best-known Bolshevik designers Dmitri Moor, Viktor Deni and the Kukriniksy Collective were as familiar with the traditional armoury of the cartoonist as they were with the language of Marx, Engels, Lenin and later Stalin. Vesyoly's poster belongs to this strain of poster-making and illustrates the proletariat posed astride the globe to terrify Western capitalists (183). German cultural critic Walter Benjamin commented in 1927 on the map as being as central to Soviet iconography as the image of Lenin, positioning capitalism in a nervous and frayed territory far out to the west.

Lenin envisaged an agitational art that could be displayed in shop windows, along public thoroughfares, in stations, at the front, and on churches and monasteries. The Bolsheviks were quick to adopt innovative strategies in order to get their message and their revolutionary language across to the people. Trains and steamships decorated with posters made them mobile and, filled with Communist agitators, their correct interpretation was ensured.

Mikhail D. Cheremnikh invented the ROSTA (Russian Telegraph Agency) window posters (179). The Moscow branch of ROSTA produced 2 million poster frames during the Civil War, and 3,100 designs for more than 450 organizations, publishing 7.5 million posters and *luboks* overall. These posters were designed under primitive conditions in response to the news as it happened and were reproduced using cardboard stencils with texts by artists such as Vladimir Mayakovsky, Osip Brik and others.

In Soviet Russia, posters provided a façade of collective solidarity based on class, labour and the authority of the Party in an effort to create a new kind of Leninist–Stalinist humanity.

CIVIL WAR IN SPAIN

Regionalism, political corruption, a powerful Catholic church, a poor education system, social inequality and a radicalized working class made Spain a melting pot of violent turmoil.

The commitment of artists and intellectuals to the Republican and anti-Fascist cause made the Spanish Civil War poster particularly vigorous. Revolutionary conditions prevailed and in Valencia, Barcelona and Madrid, printers and publishers were collectivized. Commercial and fine artists volunteered their skills for the Ministry of Propaganda and the Committee for the Defence of Madrid while the Catalan government (Generalitat) and the Press and Propaganda Department employed artists to design its posters.

The Catalan writer and poster artist Carles Fontseré described how artists' unions would meet with militias while fighting continued on the streets of Barcelona. The artists volunteered

Unknown 163 **Peace, bread. German People's Party in Bavaria** c.1920
Germany

Lucien Bernhard 164 **The German Democratic Party is the party of women** 1919
Germany

Arturo Ballester 165 **Hail to the heroes!** 1936–39
Spain

their labour and designed posters without interference from the militias, political parties or trade unions, which simply added their initials, emblems and slogans before sending them off to the presses. Designs were often selected by popular vote, and recruiting posters for the militias, and for industry and agriculture after 1937, were aimed at men, women and children in a largely illiterate and peasant society. These posters defined political territories within the cities and were seen on the streets, in shop windows, in kiosks and in town squares, on the transport system, at the front at headquarters and on bulletin boards. In his first-hand account of the Spanish Civil War, *Homage to Catalonia*, George Orwell commented that on his arrival in Barcelona, 'The revolutionary posters were everywhere, flaming from the walls in clean reds and blues that made the few remaining advertisements look like daubs of mud.'

The Spanish Republican government had little financial support from the international community and needed voluntary help from abroad. Posters emulating political photomontage in contemporary Soviet and German poster design were printed in Spanish, French and English to advertise the plight of the Republic, encouraging many volunteers from outside Spain to join the International Brigades and fight Fascism (188). These posters, and others by pre-eminent practitioners such as the Communist artist Josep Renau, illustrate the dynamics of a debate about the efficacy of a committed political art that was as aware of avant-garde, expressionist and popular models as it was of Soviet socialist realism (186).

Some artists used social realist vocabularies that had been the staple of European socialism since the 19th century and that drew upon traditional Christian iconographies. These were deployed to good effect during the war in the attack on perceived Catholic double standards (188). Some drew upon national traditions by making reference to the dual heritage of Spanish artists Velázquez and Miró (188). Communist Party posters celebrated Stalin (184), but the Republic was never seduced by the cult of the leader, and the only loyalist hero to be made iconic was the charismatic anarchist militant Buenaventura Durruti (185). A poster for the anarchist C.N.T., the largest of Spain's trade unions, deploys decorative style, fitting for an art deco ornament in a bourgeois interior (165). The art deco style was also exploited in Falangist campaigns where military authority was symbolized by the subjection of individuals to a decorative scheme in a manner often found in contemporary Nazi posters (191). Both sides used cartoon and caricature. The Republicans quite literally demonized their opponents (192), and the Francoists were identified with death, (189) in thrall to the military, capitalism, the church and German Nazism (190).

166 Above
A group of artists produce posters for the Republican war effort during the Spanish Civil War.

Heinrich Richter **167** **Three ideas: undisrupted demobilization, development of the Republic, peace** 1920
Spain

Significantly, the posters had an afterlife. Members of the International Brigades collected them and took them home, or sent them home as postcards. They were given out to visiting dignitaries by the Republican government and they were frequently reproduced in the press.

The conflict in Spain was remarkable for two things: the involvement of Fascist and Communist governments and the indecisiveness of the Western liberal democracies. For the conservative establishments in the 'non-ideological' liberal democracies the war was 'a battle of ideologies' and beyond the pale: here it quickly became a *cause célèbre* for the Left. Many civilians – men and women – volunteered for the International Brigades in support of the Republic: well-known figures such as Ernest Hemingway, Laurie Lee, André Malraux, László Rajk and Willy Brandt were among the 35,000 individuals from fifty countries. For many, it was a grand heroic gesture for humanitarian socialism, that despite the Stalinist drive to subject the Republican forces to Communist Party control, helped to sustain pro-Russian feeling (in Britain, for example), during the Second World War.

Heinz Fuchs 168 **Workers, hunger and death approach. Strikes destroy, work feeds. Do your duty, work** c.1918–19
Germany

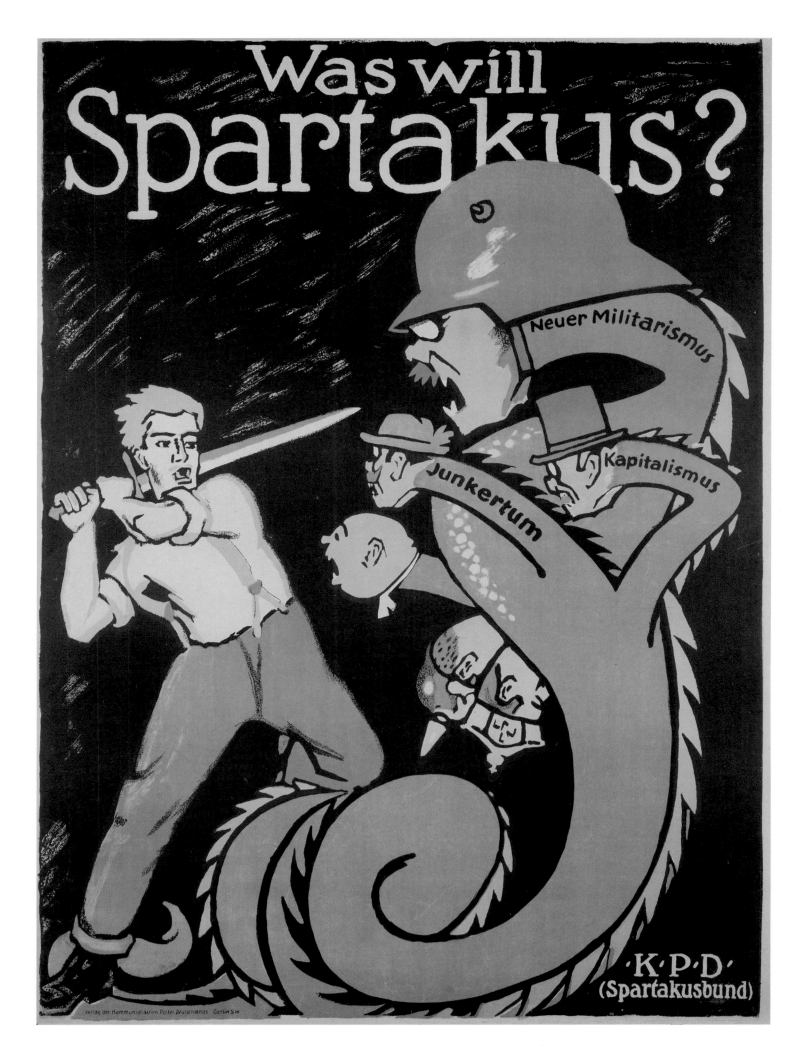

Julius Engelhard Ussy **170** **Bolshevism brings war, unemployment and starvation** 1918
Germany

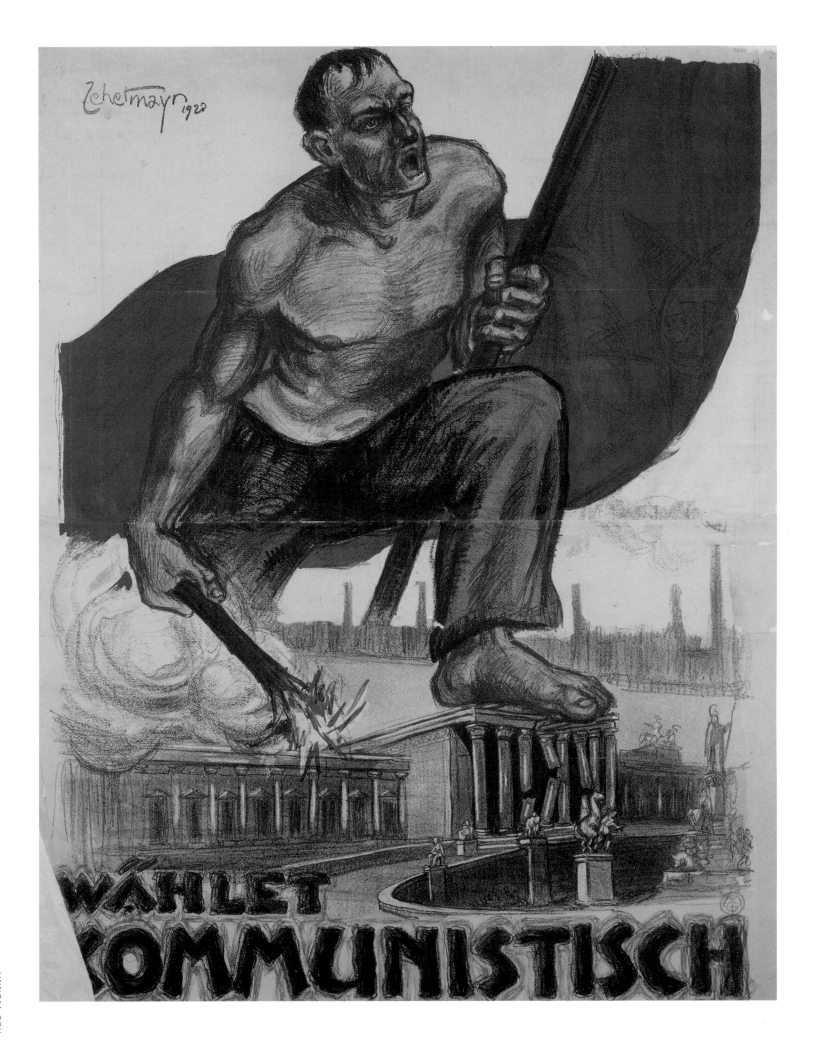

Zehet Meyer **171** **Vote Communist** 1920
Austria

Unknown 172 **This was the election result in 1919!**
Taxes. So vote Christian Socialist 1920
Austria

Bernd Steiner 173 **Vote Christian Socialist – German Christians.**
Save Austria! c.1920
Austria

174

This poster is a good example of
a designer adapting Christian iconography
to secular, political and collective ends.
Only the crown of thorns around its
ankles inhibits the march of the Christ-
like proletarian mass.

175

Mosakodnak ('they wash themselves' in
Hungarian) is used figuratively in this
context to imply trying to clear oneself
from blame. This poster is both anti-
Communist and racist: most leaders of
the Hungarian Soviet Republic, including
those of the security forces, were Jews,
and so anti-Communism was intertwined
with anti-Semitism, evident here in the
hairy outline of the man's body and his
crooked nose.

Lajos Szanto **174** **Proletarians! Forward! You shall redeem the world** c.1919
Hungary

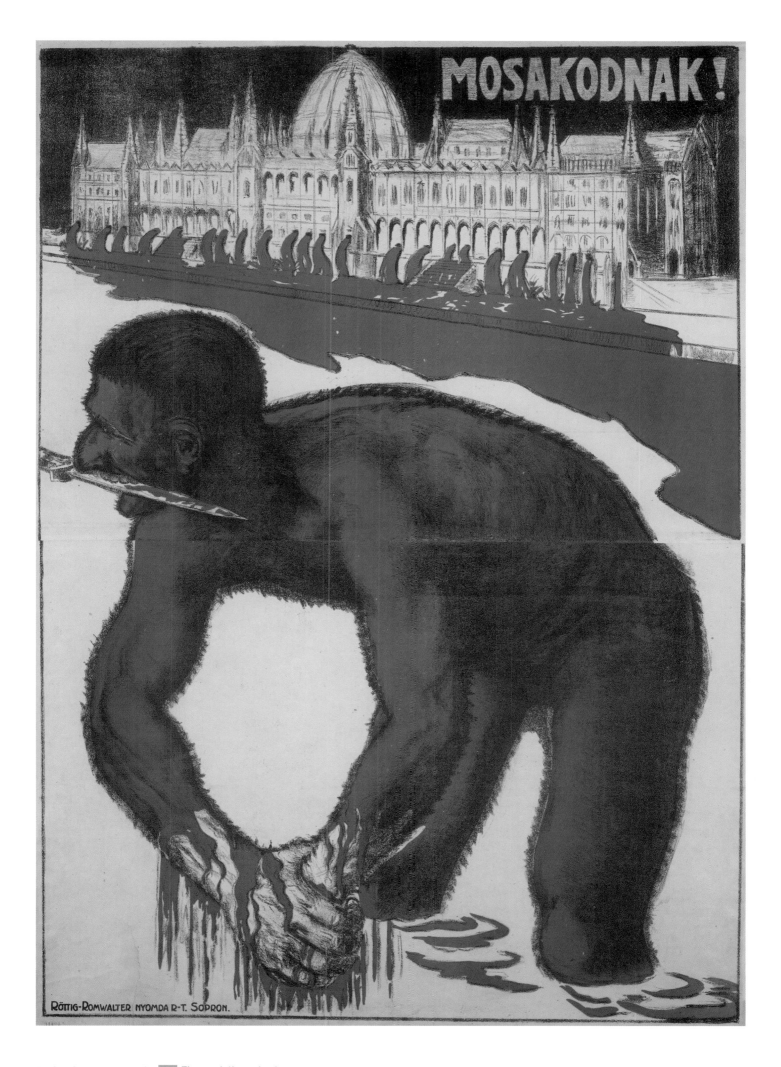

MOSAKODNAK !

Röttig-Romwalter Nyomda R-T. Sopron.

Attributed to Manno Miltiades **175** **They wash themselves!** c.1919
Hungary

Boris M. Kustodiev **176** **Freedom loan** 1917
Russia

Peter D. Butchkin 177 **Freedom loan. War until victory** 1917
Russia

Mikhail D. Cheremnikh 179 **He who is against hunger** 1920
USSR

177 Previous page
A competition was organized with
a jury chaired by Maxim Gorky to generate
posters for the Freedom Loan. Butchkin
took second place with this poster, and
Kustodiev won first prize with image 177.

180 Left
Dating from the Civil War, this poster refers
to both the White Russian armies and the
Red Army following the Russian Revolution.
The White Army is portrayed as the
defender of a unified Russia.

Unknown 180 **For one Russia. Bolshevism has encircled the heart of Russia
with a dragon** 1919
USSR

Unknown 181 **The Red Army. The defence of the proletarian
revolution** 1919
USSR

Unknown 182 **What have you done for the front?** 1920
USSR

Vesyoly 183 **Hurrah for the great anniversary! Hurrah for the fourth Congress
of the Comintern!** 1922
USSR

153

J. Briones and Jose Espert ▮184▮ **Republican Left, the Russian people help our struggle** 1937–39
Spain

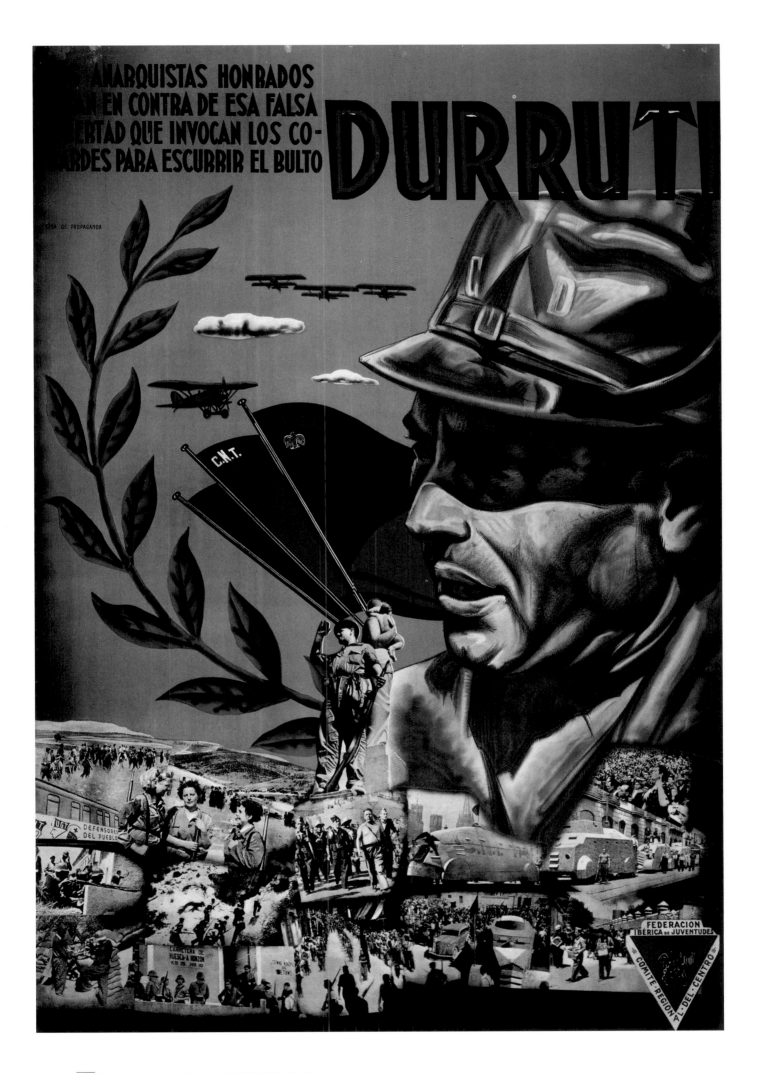

Unknown **185** **Durruti. True Anarchists are against the false liberty invoked by cowards to avoid their duty** 1936–39
Spain

185 Page 155
Buenaventura Durruti was the leader of
an Anarchist militia column, fighting
on the Republican side during the Spanish
Civil War. He died in Madrid in November
1936, shot in an accident which some
believe may have been an assassination.

189 Page 158
This anti-Fascist poster is an apocalyptic
reworking of the German Symbolist artist,
Franz von Stuck's painting, 'Der Krieg'.
Adolf Hitler was an admirer of Stuck,
believing his work embodied correct
German values. The image was also
subverted by the Dadaist artist John
Heartfield in 1933.

192 Page 161
The caption for this poster was drawn from
one of General Franco's official mottoes.
The yoke and arrows were a symbol of the
Catholic monarchs that the Spanish
Falange, the dominant Nationalist grouping
under Franco's authority, adopted as its own.

Josep Renau 186 **The farmer's produce is as sacred as the worker's wages** 1936–39
Spain

Cienas 187 **Peasants! Increase production and we crush Fascism** 1936–39
Spain

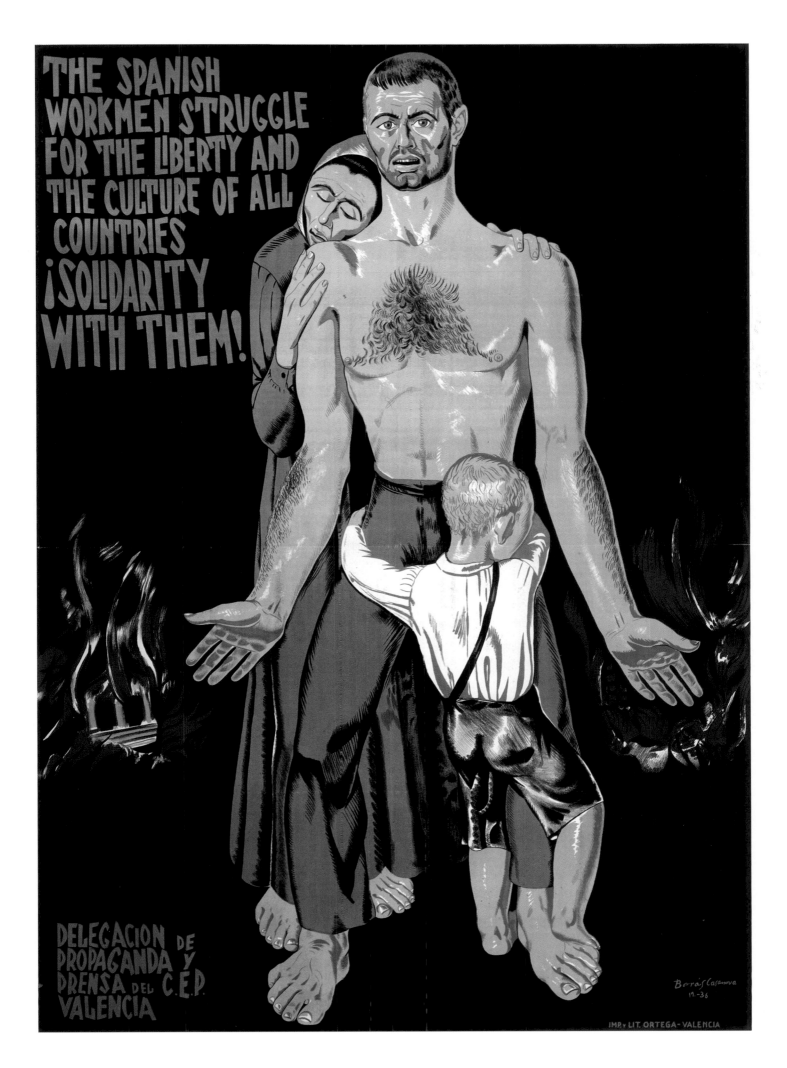

Juan Borrás Casanova 188 **The Spanish workmen struggle for the liberty and culture of all countries! Solidarity with them!** 1936
Spain

Toledo **189** **The foreign Fascist hordes attempt to invade our land. Anti-Fascists!**
Stop their march, bury them in our soil 1936–39
Spain

el generalisimo

JUNTA DELEGADA DE DEFENSA
DE MADRID

DELEGACION DE PROPAGANDA Y PRENSA

RIVADENEYRA. U.G.T.-MADRID.

SINDICATO PROFESIONALES BELLAS ARTES. U.G.T.

Pedrero **190** **The Generalisimo** 1936–37
Spain

Unknown **191 For Spain, one, great and free** 1936–39
Spain

Unknown **192** **Spain. One, great and free** 1936–39
Spain

4

The Second World War: the struggle for a brave new world

An examination of the Second World War poster reveals the relations between the communications industry and government even more clearly. Posters were openly associated with Communism in the Soviet Union and Nazism in Germany as part of the propaganda machine of the one-party state, while in the Western liberal democracies they were overtly linked to publicity campaigns. In America, in particular, posters concealed the power of the military under a rhetorical veneer of the family, working people and Roosevelt's definitions of democratic freedoms.

Posters therefore affirmed dominant values and also repressed discontent by presenting an illusion of a coherent reality. Communist and Nazi propaganda, as well as publicity in Western democracies, addressed real anxieties and feelings of dislocation. With standardized smiling people and promises of material abundance and spiritual happiness, posters were designed to give visual shape to the various social and political developments of their respective countries.

In Britain the advertising and graphic design trades dedicated themselves to the war effort and were given a large degree of autonomy in government information campaigns. The pursuit of national unity was carried out with a desire to accommodate, rather than suppress, opposition. Stylistically it was if the language of modernism had found refugee status in the design community. Posters were often executed in both art deco and abstract styles drawn from elements of commercial design in pre-war Europe. The message that wartime posters put across was a promise of greater democratic participation, education and health care – all the entitlements of citizenship that were to come true in the welfare state.

193 Opposite
This photograph by Gordon Parks was taken in 1943 and shows Union Station in Washington DC with an Office of War Information poster in the background ('Americans will always fight for liberty', also shown as poster 259 on page 203).

194 Page 164
This travel poster, produced for the German State Railways, depicts the Haus der Kunst in Munich and the Olympic Stadium in Berlin. Dominated by the Nazi eagle from Albert Speer's Reich Party Congress Grounds in Nuremberg, it was produced in Dutch, French and English language editions, and was probably made for an exhibition at the 1937 World Fair in Paris.

Richard Klein 194 **Germany's modern architecture** 1937
Germany

THE NEW ORDER: GERMANY AND OCCUPIED EUROPE
In 1934 at a Nazi Party rally in Nuremberg, Josef Goebbels
(as Minister for Public Enlightenment and Propaganda) gave
a speech in praise of propaganda. Goebbels believed propaganda
to be essential to the modern state: if threats of anarchy and
chaos were to be contained within the Nazi regime, the people
had to 'understand that the right thing is the right thing'.

The Nazi administration deployed effective marketing strategies,
and their use of the party symbol, the swastika, was a highly
successful example of branding. For example, they were careful not
to overexpose the swastika in middle-class areas until they had
seized power – not that the Social Democrats held any illusions
about the racially pure military state (217). Social realist and
expressionist graphic styles that had been exploited by leftist
parties in Europe were rejected by the Nazis in favour of art deco,
realist, illustrational styles and photographic techniques (215, 216,
219). Rather than the expression of individual suffering and doubt,
mass appeal and a certain elegance aimed at collective response
were sought after, exemplified by the work of highly successful
commercial artists such as Ludwig Hohlwein. In a 1933 issue of
the graphic design magazine *Gebrauchsgraphik*, Hohlwein asserted
the importance of commercial art in conserving cultural values
against attacks from the 'East', that is to say, anything modern,
cosmopolitan, Jewish or Bolshevik.

The advertising trade praised Hitler and Goebbels for
embodying the ideals of the nation. In 1933 the National
Socialist Federation of German Advertisers set about serving
the propaganda needs of the state, which had already made
monopolies of the radio, press, publishing, art and advertising.
Sport and the cult of youth played a large part in Nazi ideologies
of race, militarism, fitness, health and order, and were promoted on

Unknown 195 **Before: unemployment – hopelessness – waywardness
– strike – lockout. Today: work – peace – discipline –
people's comradeship** c.1934
Germany

196 **A group of young German boys view *Der Stürmer*, *Die Woche*, and propaganda posters
posted on a fence in Berlin, 1937.**

posters advertising spectacular events (219, 220), while tourism posters depicted fashionable women untouched by lipstick and powder in line with party ideology (218). In high art and architecture, the Nazis promoted Classical ideals: a travel poster featured Paul Ludwig Troost's design for the Munich art gallery, the House of German Art, as a symbol of military power and a united nation (194). The vocabularies of advertising and art were thus harnessed to the machinery of the state as well as to Nazi ideology, and it is easy to see why Walter Benjamin characterized Fascism as the 'aestheticization of politics' in his 1936 essay, 'The Work of Art in the Age of Its Reproducibility'.

The German nation was thus manipulated by advertising aimed at promoting an understanding of the war economy, ersatz goods and the need for austerity when there was little or nothing in the shops. Inevitably, by 1944 this situation had led to the collapse of the advertising trade, its dreams of finding acceptance by ruling elites unfulfilled and its role completely superseded by Nazi party propaganda.

With rallies, parades, posters and leaflets, the Nazi Party's Office for Active Propaganda aimed to create a new world view. The Nazis took a coordinated approach to propaganda, systematically exploiting events and recognizing the need for local offices throughout Germany to control the *Litfass* columns (cylindrical columns for pavement advertising), hoardings, transport systems, post offices, police stations and municipal offices (197). They regarded posters as expensive but effective, and were careful to reserve space in order to ensure the success of a campaign. By 1942 the Office for Active Propaganda had issued seven million posters in campaigns alongside radio, film and printed media. These posters portrayed large and happy families (223) and full employment (195), while radiant Nazi Youth raised funds for the cause (221, 222).

Nazi posters for the home context often appealed to historically spurious Aryan and heroic ideals of national community, whereas posters published by the Nazis in occupied Poland and Ukraine exploited Catholicism and anti-Semitism by blaming the deaths of the victims of the Stalinist Terror on a Jewish–Bolshevik conspiracy against Christianity (225). A poster from Nazi-occupied Belgium portrayed the Russian–British alliance as a Jewish conspiracy against fortress Europe (224); an example from Belgium identified the Wehrmacht and the working classes as one, in conflict with the figure of American, British, Bolshevik and Jewish capitalists (227); a Vichy French regime poster appropriates the Unknown Soldier and the memory of the First World War to declare 'Enough' as he apprehends a Jewish war profiteer and a Freemason (226); and another poster, published in Poland, adapted contemporary anti-Nazi Soviet posters (228).

197 A poster advertising the Great Anti-Bolshevism Exhibition in 1937 (*Grosse Antibolschewistiche Ausstellung*) is plastered on a *Litfass* column in Nuremberg. Photo Julien Bryan.

198 A poster of Stalin in front of the Vienna Opera, 1945.

After the defeat and surrender of the German 6th Army at Stalingrad in 1943, Nazi propaganda policy repositioned the war as a defensive struggle against Jewish–Bolshevik world domination, and occupied Europe was recast as a unified anti-Bolshevik front with the German army as its only protector (229–231). The resulting recruiting posters, designed in the style of mainstream commercial posters, betray nothing of the reality of serving in foreign SS divisions on the eastern front, or of being taken for forced labour in the Reich.

BRITAIN, EMPIRE AND A BRAVE NEW WORLD

Trained in the arts of persuasion, commercial artists saw themselves as a social necessity in wartime. In the dark days of 1942, J. B. Nicholas of the British Advertising Service Guild wrote in *Art & Industry* magazine that 'posters today are not pictures to sell pills, but to save civilization [and] however clever, are a waste of paper unless they kill Germans.' The advertising trade was under siege and this may have been little more than special pleading, but the shift to a war economy and the resulting paper shortages led to a fall in commercial advertising. Taking advantage of this situation, the government aimed to seal the link between the corridors of power and advertising that had begun in 1915.

The Ministry of Information was largely responsible for coordinating governmental campaigns and was criticized for its lack of a coherent policy. There was no unifying political line, only a liberal commonsense approach to everyday wartime necessities that soon revealed its inadequacies. Evelyn Waugh satirized the Whitehall bureaucrats responsible for this in his novel *Put Out More Flags* (1942) and their attitudes were epitomized in the correspondence, now held in the National Archives, between the Ministry and the Foreign Office concerning the first poster of the war. Designed for distribution around the Empire, this poster featured a portrait of the King in military uniform. Far from succinct, the accompanying caption used an extract from a speech delivered by the King. One exchange between the Ministry and the Foreign Office lamented the demise of Latin as a common language, while another rather more acutely pointed out that 'British freedom and democracy' did not have quite the same meaning in Whitehall as it did in the subject nations of the Empire.

The poster 'Your courage, your cheerfulness, will bring us victory' made the distinction between the ruled and the rulers, later remedied in 'Let us go forward together' (233), and other campaigns addressed wide constituencies including the Commonwealth (202, 203, 232). Post Office campaigns took a similar tack, though the modernity of the designs by F. H. K. Henrion and Pat Keely spoke for a reliance on the progressive possibilities of technology (234, 235).

G. R. Morris 202 **Join the thrift column** 1939–45
UK

C. W. Bacon 203 **England expects National Service** 1939
UK

American-inspired, large-scale exhortations with slogans such as 'Back them up!', 'Help them finish the job' or 'Mightier yet!' sustained a patronizing tone and had only a tenuous grip on reality. There was a widespread belief even within Whitehall that they were of little or no effect in Britain. Featuring images of British military hardware being put to good use in the field, they appealed to a gung-ho comic book mentality that probably held little attraction for women and certainly lacked the sophistication of some of the recruiting posters which were aimed at them.

By 1942 a pastoral chocolate-box vision of 'Little England' had gelled in the middle-class public imagination (239), which resonated with the popular and similarly unrealistic song lyric 'There'll be bluebirds over the white cliffs of Dover'. This view of Britain had developed in travel poster campaigns overseen by Frank Pick of the London Underground and Jack Beddington of petroleum company Shell-Mex Ltd, and was aided and abetted by John Betjeman's visions of England in his *Shell Guides*. All served in the wartime Ministry of Information.

199 Opposite above
A 'Wings for victory' poster hangs over part-time women war workers sorting rivets in a private home in Guildford, England, 1943.

200 Opposite centre
A row of Ministry of Information posters, Britain, 1942.

201 Opposite bottom
A view of the advertising in Piccadilly Circus, London, 1940.

203 Above
The caption for this poster is drawn from Lord Nelson's famous speech: 'England expects that every man will do his duty' during the Battle of Trafalgar in 1805.

Unknown 204 **Dig for victory** 1939
UK

205

A photograph of the 'Dig for victory' poster
displayed on Marble Arch in London (which
was used as a 'special poster site' by the
Ministry of Information). This poster campaign
(which was carried out by Charles F. Higham
Ltd) was launched at the outbreak of the war
to encourage the cultivation of gardens and
allotments. Millions of instructional leaflets
were issued and by 1943 over 1.4 million
people had allotments and were producing
over a million tons of vegetables a year.

Such campaigns relied on a patriotic belief in the common
cause and posters were intended to inform and instruct people
to radically alter their habits in order to benefit the war effort.
Posters were adapted for internal display in factories, barracks,
recruitment offices, hospitals, post offices, schools, libraries and
other civic and public institutions. Austerity took on positive
characteristics and as if to make up for wartime shortages,
posters were often decorative. Allegories were replaced by the
tangible symbols of the gear wheel, spade and kitchen table in
surprising and formally inventive combinations. Posters cajoled
the people to work hard and to a high standard, to lend and not
buy, to be economical, and to invest in the common future (242,
244–246). They encouraged hygiene, health and safety at work
and in the blackout (243, 247, 248), advised people to improvise,
grow their own food, change their diets, practise safe sex and
catch the early post (204, 205, 207, 249–253). The techniques of
surrealism, photomontage, objective realism and formal design in
various combinations created ambiguities and puns to stick in the
mind. Graphic artists such as Abram Games, Hans Schleger ('Zero'),
F. H. K. Henrion, Pat Keely and Reginald Mount were crucial in the
development of this cosmopolitan, modern and pluralistic style.
And this style owed its existence to the licence extended to the
advertising industry and to its freedom from commercial
necessities and the pressures of extreme political ideology.

Yet these devices were not appreciated by all of the design
community. J. B. Nicholas pointed out in *Art & Industry* that
while Europe crawled with millions of refugees nothing
distressing appeared in British posters. He demanded something
more virile, likening Henry Moore's well-known shelter drawings
to 'corpses in a catacomb, not cockneys in a tube' and contrasting
them to the rugged realism of First World War artists Frank
Brangwyn, Théophile-Alexandre Steinlen and Joseph Leyendecker.

Home Intelligence reports indicate that up until 1944 apathy,
self-interest and cynicism regarding British military achievements,
combined with a cautious optimism born of the limited success
demonstrated by the RAF raids over Germany, were complemented
by an overwhelming admiration for the Red Army (241). Various
'Aid Russia' campaigns attracted support (254–256) and
contributed to the development of a popular democratic socialism
that led to the Labour victory in the 1945 general election, the
harbinger of the welfare state. Abram Games expressed the
stirrings of this desire for a welfare state when he designed the
posters for the 'Your Britain, fight for it now' campaign (239,
240). These posters represented a powerful alternative to the
aspirations for a consumer paradise as promoted by the Scottish
War Savings Committee (206), but attracted criticism from the
establishment (in the form of Winston Churchill).

By the end of the war, the British poster had thus established itself in the advertising profession as an international medium capable of promoting the ideals of humanity and progress in a society that was free from the narrow nationalisms of the past.

USA AND THE FOUR FREEDOMS

Once production shifted onto a war footing following the Japanese bombing of the naval base at Pearl Harbor in 1941, artists, commercial illustrators and advertisers were perceived as superfluous in the US. Nevertheless, the curatorial and commercial sectors were supportive, and in 1941 the Museum of Modern Art (MoMA) in New York launched a competition to encourage the creation of propaganda posters in an environment free from the pressures of government or commerce (see 36, page 37).

In 1942 the War Advertising Council (WAC) developed a common cause with the Office of War Information and as a result, a group of prominent art directors was set up as the Advisory Council on Government Posters to address national problems and to help coordinate war bonds, food conservation and labour recruitment campaigns. Initially, 1.5 million copies of each major poster were printed and 10,000 messages were placed in subways, trams and buses every month: it was estimated that a billion dollars was contributed by the industry in the form of advertising space and man hours.

President Roosevelt's 1941 State of the Union Address called for the establishment of the Four Freedoms (freedom of speech and expression; freedom of every person to worship in his own way; freedom from want; and freedom from fear) as the antithesis of the New Order of tyranny. The Four Freedoms also provided the basis for advertising and industry to promote their own interests in freedom of enterprise by means of the dramatic theme of the American 'production miracle'. Advertising agents were legitimized through their sacrifices to the war effort, and as official messengers they sallied forth with their own war aims, which they inscribed on the American way of life, featuring themes such as liberty, democratic freedom, Christianity, consumer abundance and social harmony, American revolutionary history, the middle class home, the family and the virtues of free enterprise (210, 257–259).

Advertising was seen as a means of mass education and persuasion, to be deployed on behalf of American business through campaigns aimed at the public interest. In this way the industry saw itself as part of the world struggle with totalitarian tyranny. If the WAC undertook campaigns for the Treasury, tax concessions guaranteed that their finance came from the public purse, creating a mix of self-interest, patriotism, public relations and sacrifice. As expenditure on advertising rose, public service guaranteed profit.

Lowen **206** **Dreams. War savings will bring them to life** 1939–45 UK

207

A poster warning of the dangers of venereal disease is pasted to a wall outside the Ministry of Health, Westminster, London, 1943.

A migrant fruit worker from Arkansas walking by the post office, Benton Harbor, Michigan, July 1940. Photo John Vachon.

This poster was inspired by a French First World War poster by Jules Abel Faivre (113, page 97). The quotation is from John Paul Jones, a naval commander during the American revolutionary war, and his famous rebuttal to the commander of the HMS Serapis during the engagement between the Royal Navy frigate and Jones' ship Bonhomme Richard in 1779.

The US government also benefited from these campaigns. After the excesses of the First World War, the public were suspicious of government campaigns, and so Treasury Secretary Henry F. Morgenthau Jr proposed a solution in the deployment of bond publicity to support morale and to sell the idea of the war to the masses. The strategy worked on both counts. The third war loan in 1943, which was sold as an opportunity to actively participate in the war effort, was described as the 'greatest advertising operation in the history of the world'. Even more impressively, the seventh war loan in 1945 aimed to raise $14 billion but actually raised $26.3 billion.

Civic responsibility was thus subverted to a corporate end: government propaganda was privatized and the power of capital over labour was reinforced. The coercive tactics of the First World War were avoided and pictures appealing to the emotions were pitched at the lowest levels of comprehension. Design and symbolism were rejected in favour of literal photographic realism intended to 'tell the truth' (269). Even posters in heroic mode did not hesitate to list defeats (209).

Public information of this kind created a social movement that engaged all Americans: women, labour and ethnic groups – including African Americans – were enveloped by a common set of beliefs. American nationalism encouraged individualism, cultural pluralism, voluntarism and democracy, which contrasted starkly with Japanese Imperial, Nazi racial and Soviet collectivist ideologies that demanded subjection to absolute authority. This was achieved through sympathetic and realistic – although often understated and sometimes heroic representations – of the common soldier. Individuals who had made notable achievements were represented, and many of these portraits were of African Americans (262, 263) in an attempt to reach that community at a time when the armed services were segregated and African Americans were financially, socially and politically oppressed.

Unity was another major theme and posters addressed subjects such as the unity of labour and the sexes in the workplace in modern and dynamic designs heavily reliant on photography (265, 267). Inevitably, such depictions of the ordinary were supplemented by idealized Hollywood types (260, 261). Ideas of individual and heroic sacrifice, made concrete in these posters, were tied to the discourses of truth and realism associated with film. Such poster campaigns had legitimized profit and enterprise in the national cause, but their universality made demands of the population at large, mainly in terms of people's lifestyles and incomes. The reality of sacrifice for a family whose unity had survived the loss of the breadwinner is monumentalized in a studio photograph captioned 'I gave a man!' (264). The American approach involved direct and simple appeals to common lives made heroic through war.

OURS...to fight for

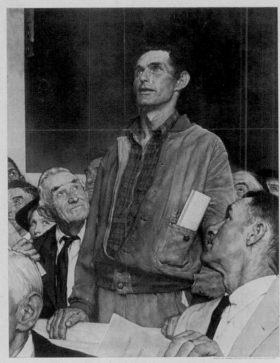

Freedom of Speech

Freedom of Worship

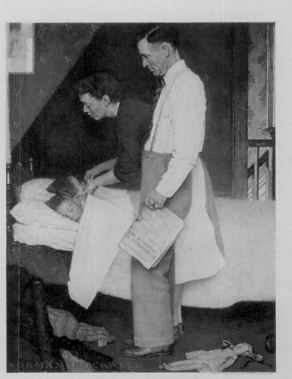

Freedom from Want

Freedom from Fear

Attributed to Harold Foster **211 Careless talk costs lives. Keep mum. She's not so dumb!** 1942
UK

Fougasse **212 Careless talk costs lives** 1942
UK

Popular opinions of organized labour and national corporations were low at the beginning of the war: work forces had been resentful of corporate power since the Great Depression of the 1930s and yet, at the same time, strikes were unpopular. It would seem that both employee and employer wanted to demonstrate their patriotism by pursuing duty rather than profit. Posters evolved accordingly, emphasizing strength, skill and unity of workers and featuring the manufacturing process, in an unconscious embodiment of 'might is right' (266). So while business and government entered the war suspicious of each other, they ended as partners: wartime campaigns succeeded in turning around the view of corporations as economically incompetent and socially irresponsible, and preserved the commercial viability of advertising to make it the voice of America.

CARELESS TALK COSTS LIVES

Security was a consistent theme for all the combatants. Fear of spies and fifth columnists was widespread and was exploited by the authorities on embattled home fronts. Ordinary situations became melodramatic and appeared full of menace: everyone, it seemed, had to be on guard against potential subversion (268). Complacency was a constant danger, and in America it was thought that using pictures showing casualties in order to generate feelings of anger could counteract this. Such a policy sat easily with governmental desire for openness (269), though outside America this direct approach was criticized for its brutality, even when, as is the case Abram Games' poster for the British army (270), it was neutralized by an abstract style.

In this narrative of trust and betrayal, the figure of the woman provided an obvious stereotype as a sexually alluring and treacherous *femme fatale* (211), the naïve 'Fashion model in denim' (271) or Fougasse's loose-lipped fishwife (212). Animal metaphors – derived from proverbs and colloquialisms – were also deployed to varying degrees of humorous effect (272, 273).

USSR AND THE NEW SOVIET PEOPLE

Under Stalin, advertising was regarded as bourgeois and wasteful, and it largely disappeared. Publicity was instead aimed at creating the new Soviet people: unalienated, collectivized and harmoniously happy citizens who were to be the antithesis of Western estranged, angst-ridden consumers. All forms of media were censored by the state and artists were controlled through the compulsory membership of official unions. During the war, the State Printing Works based in Leningrad (now St Petersburg) and Moscow published most political posters, amounting to approximately 800 designs in 34 million copies. They were distributed by party organizations who posted them in offices, canteens, workshop windows and railway stations. A mythological moral authority thus became attached to Soviet war posters; stories circulated of soldiers at the front raising them in battle and of the German command ordering them to be shot down for fear of their effect on the morale of the Russian troops.

In the 1930s, Stalin had established the cult of personality: Marx, Engels and Lenin were its ideological figureheads and their portraits appeared on posters, invariably as medallions in the sky. Stalin, on the other hand, materialized as the great helmsman, although during the war his presence was played down in favour of historical figures, the steel worker, miner, war worker, peasant and Red Army soldier with their familiar attributes of the hammer, sickle, star and red flag. Rendered heroically as idealized types in dynamic compositions, these protagonists are pitched in battle against figures of bestial Nazis and overweight capitalists.

The descendant of ROSTA (the Russian Telegraph Agency), responsible for advertising during the Russian Civil War, was TASS (Telegraph Agency of the Soviet Union), which in 1941 started a new poster campaign. Displayed mostly in shop windows, the TASS posters used simple methods of reproduction and aimed to publish within twenty-four hours of an event in runs of up to 1,000.

Ideologically, Nazism and Communism were profound enemies. So when the Nazis attacked the Soviet Union in 1941 the full weight of Soviet propaganda was turned against them. The Red Army advanced under glorious red banners and in the shadow of historical figures (276), while sturdy partisans attacked German troops from behind the lines (274). Red Army men were portrayed as victorious in mortal combat, driving the Wehrmacht beyond the Russian borders (275) and, after military success at Stalingrad, they were depicted drinking the water of the river Dnieper (282). Satirical depictions of Hitler, Goering, Goebbels and the Nazi propaganda machine had been the staple diet of Soviet poster makers since the 1930s (277–279). Later the capitalist was substituted for the Fascist beast in an iconography that persisted throughout the Cold War as the NATO countries became increasingly identified with Fascism by the Soviets.

Women were fully integrated into the Soviet war effort and depicted as the heroic embodiments of good health, happiness and productivity (280, 281). By 1949, post-war iconographies in the Soviet Union and the Communist bloc in Europe triumphantly envisioned the new Soviet people within a state-controlled aesthetic defined by Stalin's cultural henchman Andrei Zhdanov (283). The terms of Socialist Realist doctrine were optimistic and conservative and its propaganda celebrated Communist supremacy in the achievements of Yuri Gagarin and the first cosmonauts in the 1960s (284). Its founding myth was the liberation of Europe from Fascism (213) and its aim was world peace (214).

Oleg Savostyuk and Boris Ouspenskiy 213 **Glory to the heroes of the rear!** 1941–45 USSR

Unknown 214 **Nuclear explosions must be prevented from turning the beautiful into monstrosities** 1987 USSR

212 Page 172

Cyril Kenneth Bird, or 'Fougasse', was the art editor of *Punch* when the Second World War broke out, but offered his services to the British government free of charge and devoted himself to producing propaganda material. This example, which is one of a series of eight 'Careless Talk' posters, was issued by the Ministry of Information. The posters were all widely appreciated both during and after the war.

214 Page 173

In the 1980s, Soviet posters seemed to change their colour schemes from red to blue as the authorities held international poster competitions in Moscow with titles such as 'The Poster in the Struggle for Peace, Security and Cooperation'. The allegorical personification of peace as a woman would always also be read as the Rodina or Motherland.

Unknown   **215** **In the deepest need Hindenburg chose Adolf Hitler for Reich Chancellor** 1933
Germany

Unknown   **216** **All the people say yes on 10th April!** 1938
Germany

DER ARBEITER
IM REICH DES HAKENKREUZES!

DARUM WÄHLT

LISTE 1

SOZIALDEMOKRATEN!

K.GEISS.

K. Geiss 217 **The worker in the swastika state!** 1932
Germany

Hans Breidenstein (photograph by Dr Paul Wolff) **218** **North Sea resort Norderney, Prussian State resort** 1937
Germany

Ludwig Hohlwein 219 **Reichs vocational competition for German youth** 1934
Germany

Ludwig Hohlwein 220 **Reichs sports day for the League of German Maidens** 1934
Germany

Hermann Witte 221 **Build youth hostels and homes** 1938
Germany

Hermann Witte 222 **We need youth hostels** 1938
Germany

Franz Würbel 223 **Healthy parents – healthy children** 1933
Germany

Abepy 224 **Jewish conspiracy against Europe!** 1942
Nazi-occupied Belgium

Unknown 225 **And now the same fate would have awaited you** 1942
Published by the Nazis in occupied Poland and the Ukraine

Venabert 226 **Enough! Here lies a French soldier who died for the Mother Country** 1942
Vichy France

Unknown 227 **With the worker a soldier for socialism** c.1942
Nazi-occupied Belgium

226 Page 180

The French League was a right-wing organization. In order to support its own social and political agenda the League appropriated the image of the Unknown Soldier in this poster.

227 Page 180

The Allies are portrayed in this collaborationist poster as the embodiment of an international Jewish conspiracy, in a contradictory amalgam of Capitalism and Communism. The overriding theme is common to propaganda produced in all German-occupied countries: an interpretation of the positive effects of a united Europe under National Socialism.

228 Page 181

This is a Nazi poster designed to recruit Ukrainian nationals to the Galicia Division in order to fight with the German Army on the eastern front.

229 Above left

The SS Volunteer Panzer-Grenadier Brigade 'Nederland' was formed in Spring 1943. It only ever recruited about 2,500 members, and half of its complement was lost in the 'battle of the European SS' at Narva, Estonia, in July 1944.

Unknown **229** **Netherlanders: for your honour and conscience! Against Bolshevism** 1943
Nazi-occupied Holland

Unknown **230** **Your place is still vacant in the Waffen SS** 1942
Nazi-occupied Holland

EN TRAVAILLANT EN ALLEMAGNE
tu seras l'Ambassadeur de la
QUALITÉ FRANÇAISE

Attributed to Raoul Eric Castel **231** **While working in Germany you will be the ambassador of French quality** 1943
Vichy France

THE BRITISH COMMONWEALTH OF NATIONS

TOGETHER

233 Opposite
The caption for this poster is taken from Winston Churchill's first speech as Prime Minister to the House of Commons on 13 May 1940, which was later known as 'Blood, Toil, Tears and Sweat'.

"LET US GO FORWARD TOGETHER"

F. H. K. Henrion 234 **We're in it together** 1943
UK

Pat Keely 235 **Wireless war** 1943
UK

AFS

ARP   LCC

WOMEN REQUIRED
FOR MOTOR DRIVING
& TELEPHONIST DUTIES
APPLY ANY FIRE STATION

COSMO CLARK

John Cosmo Clark 236 **Women required for motor driving and telephonist duties** c.1941
UK

Philip Zec **237 Women of Britain come into the factories** 1941
UK

Jonathan Foss **238 Serve in the WAAF with the men who fly** 1941
UK

Tcp: Frank Newbould **239** **Your Britain. Fight for it now** 1942
UK

Above: Abram Games **240** **Your Britain. Fight for it now** 1942
UK

239 Opposite above

**This poster was one of several produced
to promote a traditional pastoral image
of Britain.**

240 Opposite below

**One of a series of three posters on health,
housing and education. The fusion of
bombsite with modern concrete
architecture (the building is Berthold
Lubetkin's Finsbury Health Centre) show
familiarity with European modernism.
Winston Churchill objected to the child
with rickets and the poster was withdrawn
after initial distribution to the army and
its display at Harrods Poster Exhibition.**

Sevek **241** **On to Japan!** 1945
UK

His needs come first: Lend-don't spend
POST OFFICE SAVINGS BANK

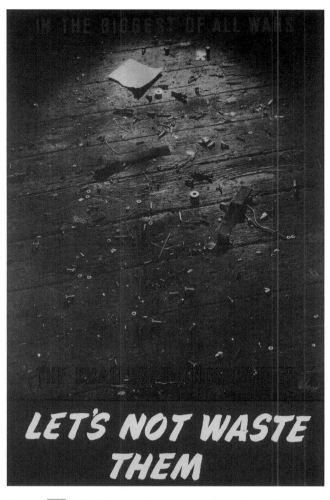

Unknown `243` **In the biggest of all wars the smallest things matter** 1939–45
UK

Pat Keely `244` **Full ahead – production** 1943
UK

Unknown `245` **Smooth finish. Perfect flight** 1939–45
UK

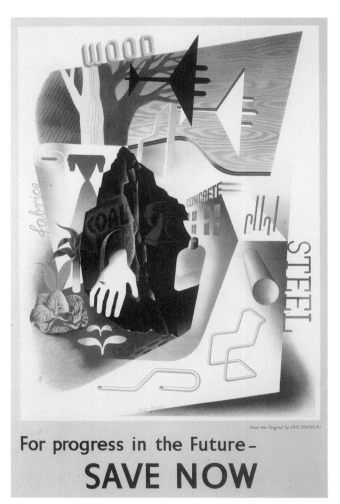

Eric Fraser `246` **For progress in the future. Save now** 1944–45
UK

Abram Games **247** **This child found a 'blind'** 1943
UK

G. R. Morris 248 **Wait! Count 15 slowly before moving in the blackout** 1939–41
UK

195

Hans Schleger ('Zero') 249 **Eat greens for health** 1939–45
UK

Abram Games 250 **Grow your own food** 1942
UK

George Him and Jan Le Witt 'Lewitt-Him' **251** **Post early, and don't miss the 'noon' post** 1941–42
UK

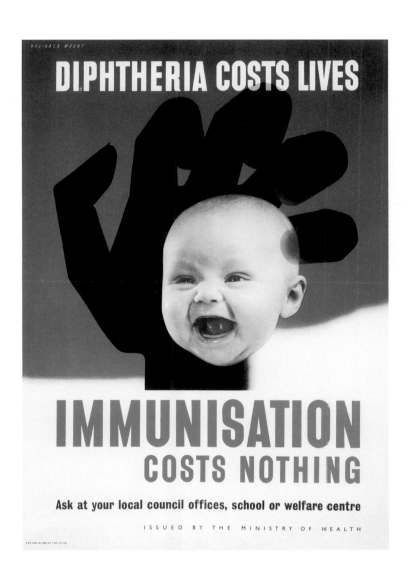

Reginald Mount 252 **Diphtheria costs lives. Immunisation costs nothing** 1943
UK

Reginald Mount 253 **VD hello boyfriend coming 'MY' way?** 1943–44
UK

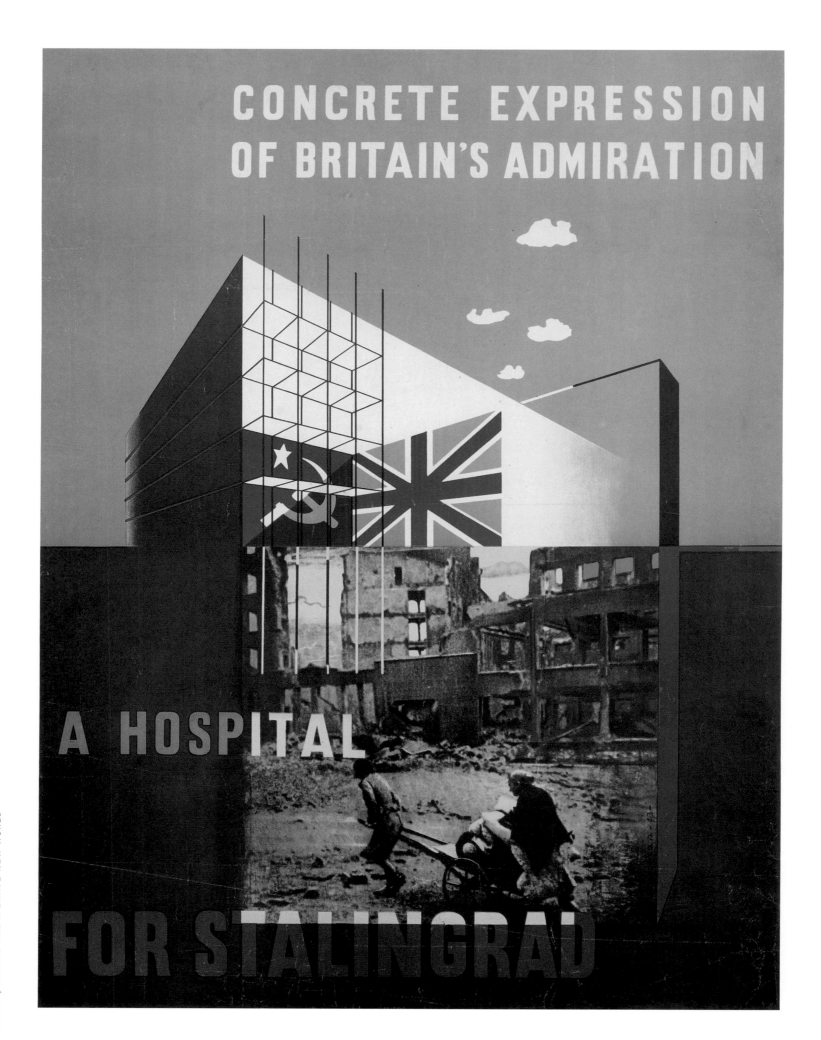

CONCRETE EXPRESSION OF BRITAIN'S ADMIRATION

A HOSPITAL FOR STALINGRAD

255 Above
This image was 'No. 5' in a series (the others included a tank, lorry and parcels), designed to be sent to the Soviet Union to highlight British aid.

Reginald Mount 255 **From the British people** 1941
UK

F. H. K. Henrion 256 **Aid the wounded. Red Army day** 1942
UK

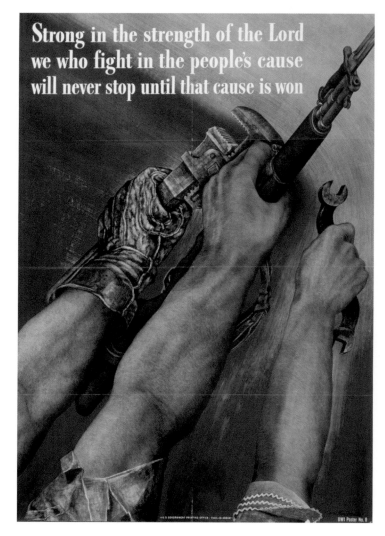

257 Above left

The quote on this poster is taken from
US President Abraham Lincoln's 1863
Gettysburg Address – one of the most
quoted, and most famous, speeches in
American history. It was delivered during
the American Civil War, four and a half
months after the Union armies defeated
the Confederates at the decisive Battle
of Gettysburg.

258 Above right

This quote is also taken from a famous
American speech, this time from US Vice
President Henry Wallace's 1942 speech
to the Free World Association in New York
City. Grounded in Christian references,
Wallace laid out a positive vision for the
war beyond the simple defeat of the Nazis.

259 Opposite

This poster shows American GIs taking
inspiration from their revolutionary
forefathers at Valley Forge in 1778 during
the American War for Independence.

Allen Saalberg 257 **Remember Dec. 7th!** 1942
USA

David Stone Martin 258 **Strong in the strength of the Lord** 1942
USA

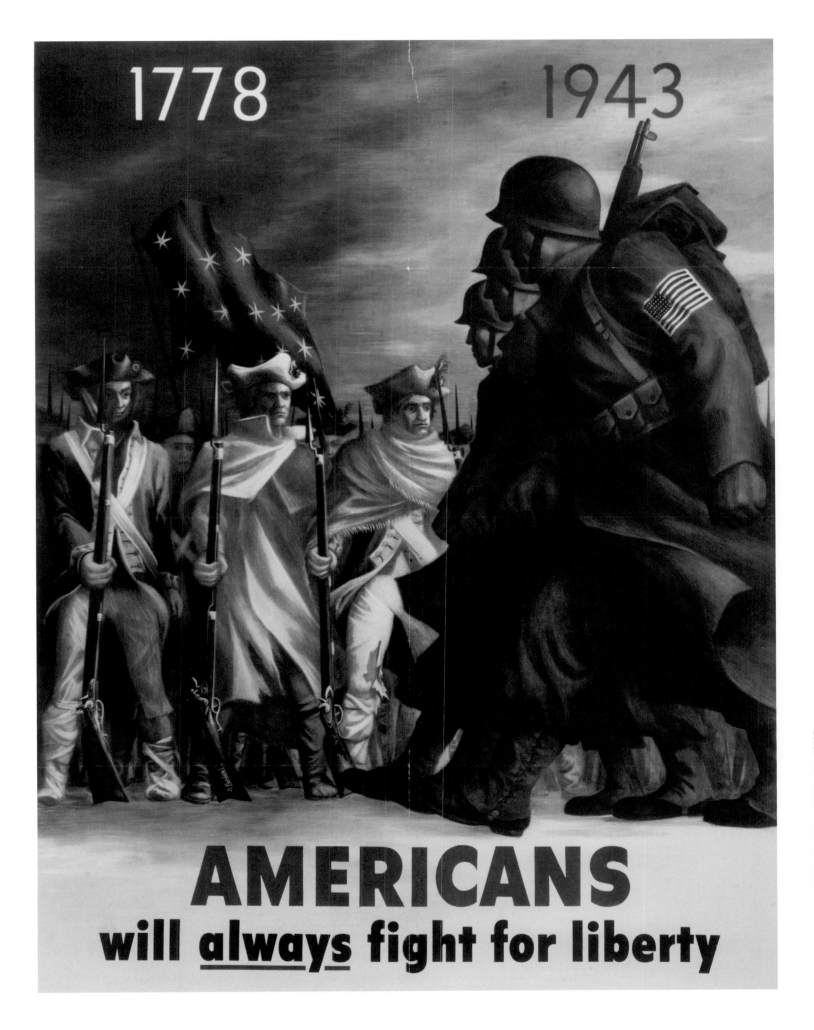

1778 1943

AMERICANS
will <u>always</u> fight for liberty

Bernard Perlin 259 Americans will always fight for liberty, 1778–1943 1943
USA

Carolyn Moorehead Edmundson **260** **Enlist in a proud profession! Join the US Cadet Nurse Corps** 1942
USA

262 Below left
Navy chef Dorie Miller won the Navy Cross at Pearl Harbor. This poster commemorates his actions as 'above and beyond the call of duty', thereby embracing the African American community in the war effort.

263 Below right
The portrait of Robert Diez in this poster celebrates his ninety-three successful missions over North Africa and Italy with the 99th Pursuit Squadron made up of African Americans.

David Stone Martin 262 **Above and beyond the call of duty** 1943
USA

Unknown 263 **Keep us flying! Buy war bonds** 1943
USA

Valentino Sarra 264 **I gave a man!** 1942
USA

Unknown 265 **Women in the war. We can't win without them** 1942
USA

Unknown 266 **Buy a share in America** 1942–45
USA

UNITED WE WIN

OWI PHOTO BY LIBERMAN

WAR MANPOWER COMMISSION • WASHINGTON, D. C.

Unknown (photograph by Howard Liberman) **267** **United we win** 1942
USA

Unknown 268 **The enemy is listening in!** 1943
Germany

Herbert Morton Stoops 269 **Careless talk ... got there first** 1944
USA

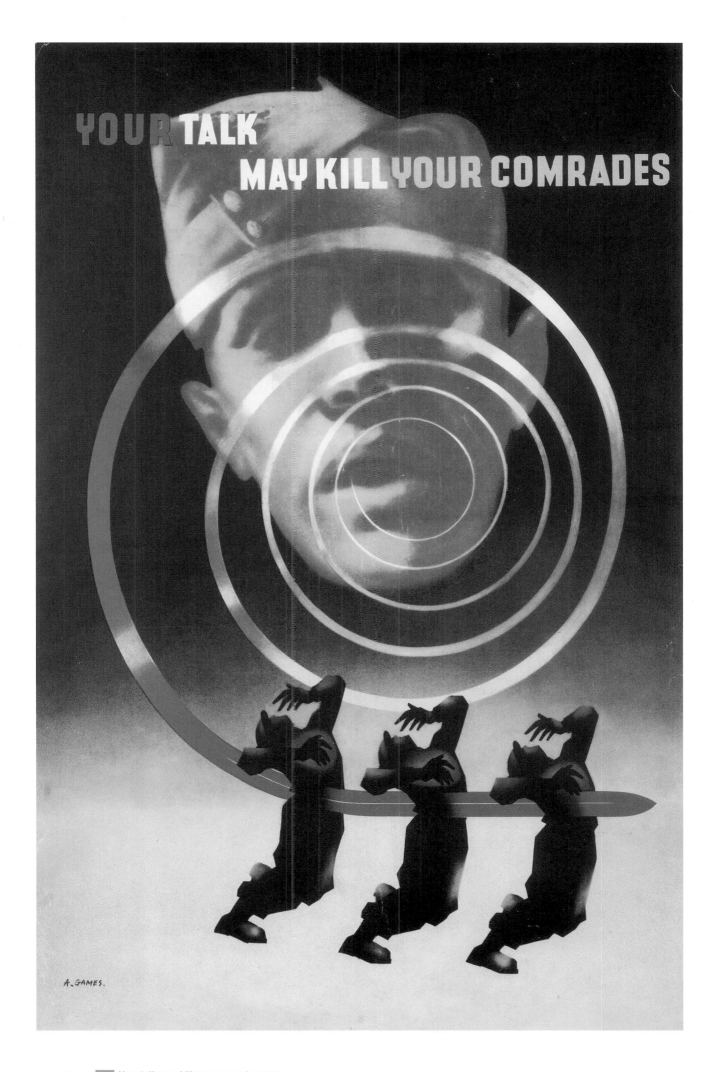

Unknown 271 **Be careful what you say or write, 'PLEASE, get there ... and back!** 1942
USA

Unknown 272 **Shame on you, chatterbox! The enemy is listening.
Silence is your duty** 1943
Germany

Unknown 273 **Don't be a sucker! Keep your mouth shut** 1942–45
USA

The group comprised three artists:
Mikhail Kuprianov, Porfiri Krylov and
Nikolai Sokolov. On Hitler's invasion,
Stalin put less emphasis on Party
propaganda and looked instead to
historical precedents. Suvorov was
an 18th-century Russian general who
never lost a battle; Chapayev was
a hero of the Civil War.

A favourite device of Soviet satirists
was to compare the likely fate of Hitler
in Russia to that of Napoleon.

Top: Kukryniksi Group **276** **We're daring and skilful in combat. We're Suvorov's descendants, Chapayev's children** 1941 USSR

Above: Kukryniksi Group **277** **Napoleon failed and so will the conceited Hitler!** 1941 USSR

N. Shukov and Viktor Semenovich Klimashin **278** **Beat the German beasts! The destruction of Hitler's army is possible and necessary** 1943
USSR

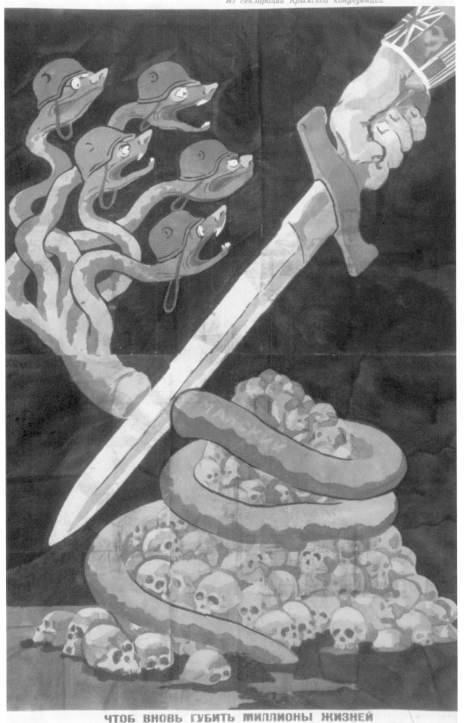

P. Sarkisyn 279 **Let's kill the hydra!** 1941–45
USSR

ОКНО ТАСС № 699

САЛЮТ ГЕРОЯМ!

Вперед, вперед!.. Как близки нам названья
Отбитых сел, и рек, и городов!
И тот, кто знал всю горечь расставанья,
Теперь запеть от радости готов.

И сил как-будто сразу больше стало.
Готов работать, не смыкая глаз,
Чтоб завтра вновь, как песня, прозвучал он,
Победный, гордый, Сталинский Приказ.

художник — В. ИВАНОВ   текст — В. ЛЕБЕДЕВ-КУМАЧ

282 Opposite below
**This poster makes direct reference
to the defeat of the German 6th Army
at Stalingrad.**

284 Page 219
**The poster welcomes the visit of two
Soviet cosmonauts to East Berlin.**

Mikhail Alexandrovich Gordon, 281 **Victory is close at hand! More help to the front** 1945
L. H. Orekov and A. G. Petrov   USSR

Viktor Ivanov 282 **We're drinking water from the native Dnieper.
We'll drink from the Prut, Nieman and Bug! Let's
clear the Soviet land of the Fascist scum!** 1943
USSR

1. MAI 1953

Unknown 283 **1 May 1953** 1953
German Democratic Republic

HERZLICH WILLKOMMEN

Unknown **284 A hearty welcome** 1961
German Democratic Republic

5

The Cold War and the New World Order

Partly stimulated by the virulent anti-Communism of the 1950s, the American way of life came under simultaneous assault from groups dedicated to social change and the protection of civil liberties on the one hand, and a youth-orientated consumer culture on the other. On both sides of the Cold War divide, official political rhetoric propagandized in favour of democracy. But political culture in post-war America and the Soviet Union seemed to hold that domination was necessary for self-determination, repression was a condition of freedom, privilege was a prerequisite of equality, and humanitarianism justified human rights abuses. The political climate therefore inevitably carried with it the seeds of its own destruction, or at least ill repute, and was perhaps most adequately summed up in the Vietnam era graffiti: 'Fighting for peace is like fucking for virginity'.

Eventually, in the West, these pressures gave rise to new social movements, all of which challenged patriarchal and state structures, and with varying degrees of success struggled for cultural autonomy and resisted appropriation by commerce. Necessarily operating outside the mainstream, the poster was an important means of expression in this political climate and, as a relatively cheap medium, was suited to the protest march, fly-posting, hand-to-hand distribution and the noticeboard. Moreover, posters projected cultural perspectives that challenged the dominant views expressed in film, on television, in the newspapers and on the hoardings, which remained the preserves of state and capital.

PEACE MOVEMENT
In Western Europe the intellectual Left took a progressively anti-American stance in its pursuit of world peace, freedom of expression and the status of the individual. Partly encouraged by Communist propaganda peace initiatives, public figures such

Anti-war protesters prepare to topple a statue of President Bush, London, 20 November 2003.

ST P
BU$H
TIM 4 PEAC
GO!
MAB
END
OCCUPATION
OF
IRAQ
Troops out now

Unknown 286 **Let us take the risks of peace upon ourselves, not impose the risks of war upon the world** c.1965
UK

Ian MacLaren 287 **Easter March** 1966
UK

as actor Paul Robeson, artist Rockwell Kent and world-famous scientist Albert Einstein campaigned with Pablo Picasso's 'Dove of Peace' as their emblem (286). In 1956 following Soviet leader Khrushchev's 'secret speech' (in which he denounced the 'cult of personality' surrounding Stalin, accusing him of crimes committed during the Great Purges in the 1930s) and the Soviet invasion of Hungary, Communist influence was seriously compromised. In America, the issue of nuclear weapons and what US president Eisenhower described as the dangers of the American 'military–industrial complex' remained in place. Partly in response to this situation, a group of influential British figures including historians and philosophers E. P. Thompson, A. J. P. Taylor, Michael Foot and Bertrand Russell founded the Campaign for Nuclear Disarmament (CND) in 1958. Designed by Gerald Holtom, CND's emblem was based on the semaphore signals for 'N' and 'D', and has since become a universal peace sign.

The abstract design of early posters during this period signified the peaceful use of nuclear technology and echoed the post-war modernism found in international exhibitions such as the Brussels World Fair (1958) or the Soviet Exhibition in Paris (1961) (286, 287). But this approach was compromised on two levels. Firstly, it was a style adapted to commodities that consumers associated with the American way of life. Secondly, advanced technology was increasingly exploited by the defence industry, a fact underscored by the use of an intercontinental ballistic missile to launch Yuri Gagarin, the first astronaut, into orbit. In other words, there was no easily available graphic language of opposition within popular culture of the day: in the Communist world it was illegal, and in the West there was no market to support it.

Later poster designs used the mushroom cloud of nuclear Armageddon as a principal motif within stark compositions. Well-known designers such as F. H. K. Henrion and Peter Kennard contributed graphics on both sides of the Atlantic, illustrating the depth of support felt within the design community across the world. Many of these posters were small-scale and monochrome or used single-spot colour, and were functional rather than decorative (297–300).

With the deployment of Soviet SS-20 nuclear missiles in the 1980s, and NATO's counter deployment of Pershing and Cruise missiles in Europe, the peace movement looked again to resurrect discussion with its supporters in Communist Europe. Germany was the possible nuclear battlefield and posters in East Germany were schematic and unequivocal in their condemnation of NATO (302, 304). Conversely, Peter Kennard's photomontages for the British Labour Party and CND adapted the contemporary symbolism of international Communism's propaganda for peace (303).

It is worth reiterating that poster designers on both sides of the Cold War divide often engaged with social themes. This was especially evident from the 1960s onwards, in the international poster biennales in Brno, Warsaw and Chaumont. In the devastation of the Second World War and its aftermath, organizations such as the Alliance Graphique Internationale and later the International Council of Graphic Design Associations promoted good design with the goal of creating a better society. Likewise, under the category of the 'social poster', international artists produced designs in small or even unique editions destined for exhibition. Adopting this late modernist agenda, some artists and designers were able to successfully circumvent political censorship in Prague following the invasion of Czechoslovakia in 1968, and also at the collapse of Communism in 1989. One of István Orosz's posters, for example, commemorated the departure of the Soviet Army from Hungarian soil, and functioned in several different versions as both an 'exhibition' poster and as an 'election' poster for one of the newly founded political parties in Hungary (288).

VIETNAM

By 1968, American involvement in Vietnam had become a focus for discontent. The American anti-war movement gained momentum as a result, drawing strength from the Civil Rights and Peace and Free Speech movements. It found a voice in alternative styles of behaviour, dress, music and underground graphics in America and Europe: affiliation with the counterculture effectively became a lifestyle statement rather than a thoroughgoing political position.

Small presses proliferated and posters subverted national symbols, much as press cartoonists had throughout the era (see 19 on page 23, 304, 305). New heroes such as the Marxist revolutionary Che Guevara provided the peace movement with

István Orosz 288 **Comrades it's over** 1990 Hungary

288 Above

Orosz produced this poster in a number of different versions to celebrate the withdrawal of the Soviet Army from Hungarian soil to campaign for one of the first independent democratic parties after the end of Communist rule (as illustrated here) and to condemn the re-election of the Communist Party in 1995 with the caption 'I'm back again!'.

289 Left

An anti-Vietnam War protest outside the US embassy in Grosvenor Square, London on 27 October 1968.

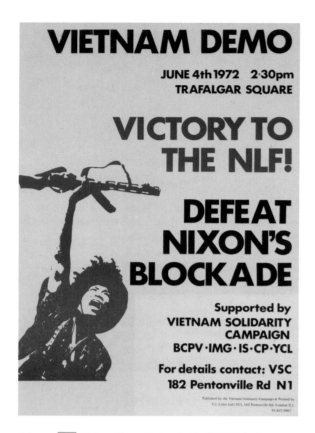

Unknown 290 **Vietnam Demo. Victory to the NLF! Defeat Nixon's blockade** 1972
UK

iconic symbols, and simultaneously became increasingly popular with a growing international youth market: in America alone, art historian David Kunzle estimated in his book *Art as a Political Weapon* that between 20,000 and 40,000 different poster designs were produced during the period 1965–75. Many such posters used the war as a vehicle to attack American values of hard work, but scores of the more elaborate designs were destined for adornment of the bed-sit wall, the student common room, the commune and the 'head shop', and established symbols for what later became known as an alternative lifestyle (306).

If posters are 'weapons' as is sometimes claimed, some are more lethal than others. Small, cheaply printed monochrome designs were created specifically for guerrilla posting or parading on political demonstrations (307, 309), though the latter purpose was more often served by handmade placards showing simple slogans (289). Posters announcing demonstrations were crudely designed, used minimal graphics and sometimes adopted the heroic iconographies of the 'enemy' as a register of their opposition (290, 309).

'Q. And babies? A. And babies', using a photo taken by Ronald Haeberle, was originally published as an anonymous collaboration that was in tune with the political tenor of the time (see 29, page 31). This poster took its caption from an interview with an American soldier who had participated in the massacre of Vietnamese civilians at My Lai in 1968. The original distributors at MoMA, New York, refused to publish the poster, and it was instead taken up by the Art Workers' Coalition who demonstrated with it in the museum, in front of Picasso's famous painting 'Guernica' (inspired by the Nazi bombing of the Spanish town of Guernica in 1937) and published 50,000 copies for worldwide distribution (291). This was a severe and telling indictment of American foreign policy that few could ignore.

291 Right
The Art Workers' Coalition (AWC) and the Guerilla Art Action Group protest in front of Picasso's 'Guernica' at the Museum of Modern Art, New York, with the AWC's 'Q. And babies? A. And babies?' poster, 8 January 1970.

NORTHERN IRELAND

Contemporary posters in Northern Ireland were of a rather different kind. The violence and unrest involving Republican and Loyalist paramilitary organizations, the Royal Ulster Constabulary (RUC), the British Army and others in Northern Ireland between the late 1960s and late 1990s (often referred to as 'The Troubles') owed their origins to the Catholic community's desire for full political enfranchisement. The Northern Ireland Civil Rights Association campaigned for the Catholic community and, in emulation of the American Civil Rights movement, organized marches, pickets, sit-ins and protests that aimed to pressurize the government of Northern Ireland to prevent the gerrymandering of district councils and end discriminatory laws, policing, housing and employment policies. The British Army was sent into Northern Ireland by the British government to protect the Catholic community against Protestant paramilitaries. But army tactics and the imposition of internment in 1971 by the British government alienated the civilian population in Republican areas, and the Irish Republican Army (IRA) and other political groupings on the extreme left turned against the army as colonial occupiers (310–313).

Posters could have only a limited effect on a population divided along sectarian lines, controlled by army roadblocks and military watchtowers, and segregated geographically. In a province marked by sectarian murals, official posters that encouraged people to help stop the violence could hardly venture beyond unemployment offices, police stations and government buildings. Implicit visual references to the bombing of Guernica by the Nazis during the Spanish Civil War identified the IRA with Fascist crimes (314); other posters used text to directly accuse the IRA of murder in order to reiterate the British government's refusal to give terrorists any political status.

Many posters created within the Catholic and Protestant communities were handmade with stencils or crude screens and were not designer objects, still less lifestyle statements. Small in scale, easy to conceal from the authorities and to fly-post onto any available space, they were primarily made to inform the public of demonstrations, and to reaffirm political territories.

THE NEW WORLD ORDER

Posters are part of our urban fabric today, and they are particularly successful when the power they represent becomes invisible within common culture and everyday life. The values of the mainstream media dedicated to the buying and selling of commodities and certain authorized political, social and economic opinions can dominate the public sphere to limit political participation.

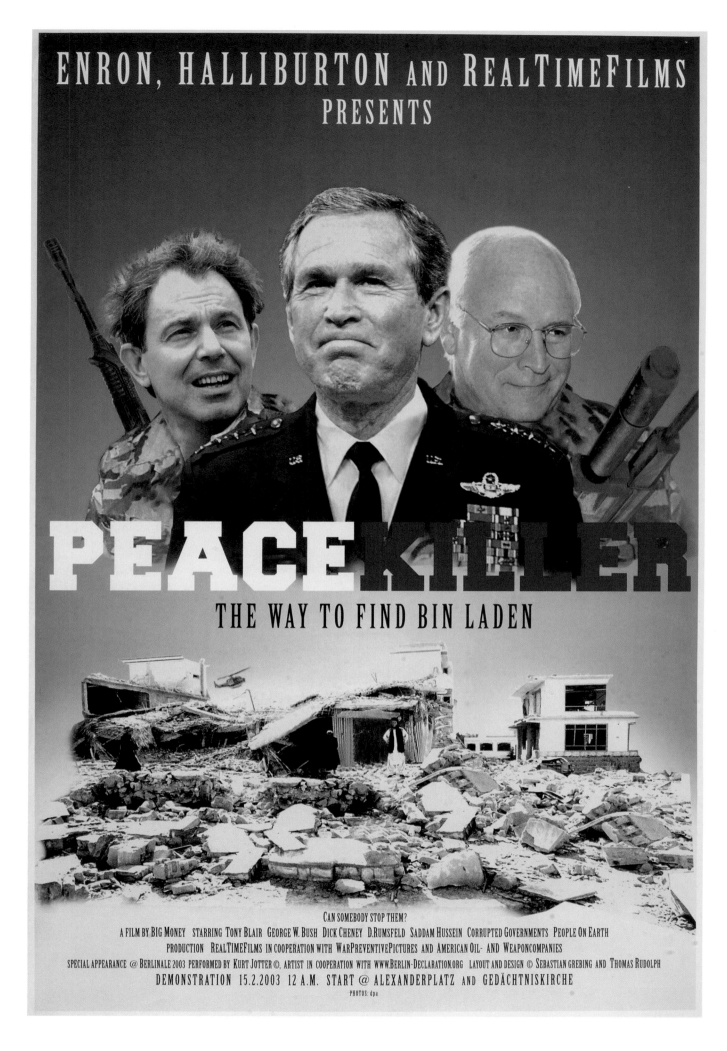

Kurt Jotter, Sebastian Grering and Thomas Rudolph **292** **Peace killer. The way to find Bin Laden** 2003
Germany

As discussed earlier in this book, it could be argued that the collapse of Communist authority in the late 1980s and early 1990s briefly generated what German sociologist Jürgen Habermas described in his book *The Structural Transformation of the Public Sphere* as a liberal or public sphere, where rational debate could transcend self or vested interests in civil society. This has, arguably, been repeated on a much smaller scale in Israel from the early 1980s. David Tartakover produced original designs to promote Yesh Gvul – which translates as 'There is a limit!' or 'There is a border' – a leftist movement within the Israeli Defence Force dedicated to ending the repressive policies of the Israeli government in the occupied territories (315). In 2003, American intellectual and activist Susan Sontag remarked in her keynote speech at the Oscar Romero human rights award ceremony for Ishai Menuchin, chairman of Yesh Gvul:

> 'We are all conscripts in one sense or another. For all of us, it is hard to break ranks; to incur the disapproval, the censure, the violence of an offended majority with a different idea of loyalty. We shelter under banner-words like justice, peace, reconciliation that enroll us in new, if much smaller and relatively powerless communities of the like-minded; that mobilize us for the demonstration, the protest, the public performance of acts of civil disobedience not for the parade ground and the battlefield.'

Activists elsewhere, using affirmative and repetitive marketing techniques, employed alternative means in order to engage the passive consumer. The stand against the iconography of the media – as defined in Second World War discourses on the American way of life, Hollywood and branded goods – intuitively recognized the weakening of the public sphere. Vocabularies established in the First World War, which offered an easy alliance of tobacco and beef extract in support of the national cause, were now superseded by the subversion of branded goods produced by international corporations (292, 295, 316–318).

What became known as a 'culture-jamming' community evolved in the 1990s, addressing American foreign policy and economic interests rather than those of freedom and democracy in advertising and publicity. This phenomenon was a sign of the compromising of politics by consumer culture, which was most notably exposed in the McLenin parody of the McDonalds' logo (featuring Lenin's head superimposed on the company logo) found on tourist t-shirts in the wake of the collapse of Communism in Russia in the early 1990s.

We have seen how illusion, manipulation and some resistance marked out a separation in the public sphere between those defined as consumers, voters, clients or customers, who are

293 Above
A member of the Stop the War organization prepares signs in London on 17 November 2003 ahead of massive street protests planned during US President George W. Bush's state visit to Britain. The protesters are demanding that US and British troops leave Iraq.

292 Opposite
This poster makes references to Halliburton – one of the largest US civilian contractors in Iraq – and its connections to US Vice President Dick Cheney.

Adam Nieman **294** **B52-State sponsored terrorism** 2003
UK

Micah Ian Wright **295** **Join the army … Vacancies available** 1999–2007
USA

recognized and represented, and those belonging to any of the various subcultures in society who are not. This was emphasized in government legislation and George Bush's declaration of a 'War on Terror' in the wake of the 9/11.

New forms of technology have to some extent transformed the appearance of the public sphere as we know it today. Initially mobile phones enabled rapid organization for intervention in public affairs. Then web-based organization developed in Seattle in 1999, when anti-globalization protesters used the internet to coordinate demonstrations during the World Trade Organization meeting of world leaders. The internet provides cheap and easy dissemination, and where fly-posting is illegal, it allows people to access material in the comfort of their homes or internet cafés and libraries. More significantly, the internet allows protest movements to coordinate simultaneous protests around the globe in order to create spectacles on a scale comparable to the carefully orchestrated advertising campaigns of global brands. The 'Stop the war against Iraq' protests in Britain in February 2003, for example, were the largest the country had ever seen and were relatively sparsely seeded with protest posters, simply because the speed of events had run ahead of production capacity. Subsequent marches were increasingly 'armed' with posters as organizations alongside the Stop the War Coalition, such as the Socialist Workers Party and Respect, set out to exploit the situation by supplying posters for marchers to carry.

The spread of access to the internet has also encouraged e-activism. Sites dedicated to a particular cause, such as opposition to the war in Iraq, can put out a PDF of a poster or a flyer on their websites for people to download and make their own copies from. Individual artists such as Adam Nieman have even put up their own sites (294). Others are dedicated to the free distribution of anti-war graphic material and define their role within a liberal individualist notion of the artist as a radical and social critic: 'As creative individuals trained in methods of mass communication, we can make a real difference by providing clear anti-war messages,' suggests ANTI-WAR.US. This site, unlike others, does not sell its material to its customers: posters are instead 'created voluntarily and distributed free to activists around the world'. Many graphic artists go one step further, creating satirical designs and sending them to their contacts as attachments, which then spread exponentially around the globe.

The Stop the War Coalition founded in Britain in September 2001 is a typical example of an organization with a political agenda that has embraced e-activism. The coalition questions the validity of the so-called 'War on Terror', opposes the war in Afghanistan and the occupation of Iraq, embraces moderate Muslim organizations, promotes anti-racism and defends civil liberties. It is uncontaminated by established party politics and has no political programme, acting in the name of humanitarianism as embodied in posters by artists such as David Gentleman, Clifford Harper, Ralph Steadman, Leon Kuhn, Peter Kennard, Jamie Reid and Steve Bell (see 1, page 6, 319–322). Design agency Karmarama also produced posters for the Stop the War coalition, although it has, in addition, produced designs for retail, commercial and political bodies such as Selfridges, Ikea, Amnesty International and the British Conservative Party.

At the beginning of the 21st century, governments still use posters to promote their agendas, but without the grandiose propaganda ends in mind that were common during the First and Second World Wars, now that recruiting is discreet and war loans unnecessary. Similarly, charities and non-governmental organizations pursue their goals through different mechanisms such as television campaigns and mailings. The poster dedicated to political ideology and personal commitment, however, has increasingly found a home with groups and organizations seeking social change through opposition to official government and corporate policies.

In the post-war world, the state capitalism of the Soviet sphere of influence and the corporate capitalism of Western democratic liberalism articulated messages in a distinctive visual rhetoric, which was a step removed from reality. But with the failure of Communist and consumer utopias, and their visual rhetorics turned in against themselves on both sides of the former Iron Curtain, brand subversion and humanitarian opposition to official government policy became the order of the day. In this, the politics of the street have been helped by the development of the internet, where virtual space has become a territory as important as any physically 'real' public space. So in this sense propaganda and publicity have been revived as the positive social force they were originally intended to be, in a context free from government, corporate advertising and commerce: the web enables protest to circumvent, and to an extent undermine, established political and media structures.

295 Opposite below
This propaganda remix project subverts historical war posters: the original 1943 poster designed by John Atherton carried the caption 'a careless word...another cross' (see page 5).

296 Below
Women bearing red flags parade through Red Square in Moscow, during the 1979 celebrations to commemorate the 59th anniversary of the October Revolution. The poster reads: 'Communist party of the Soviet Union. The party leads us to Communism!'

Unknown **297** **NO** c.1972
UK

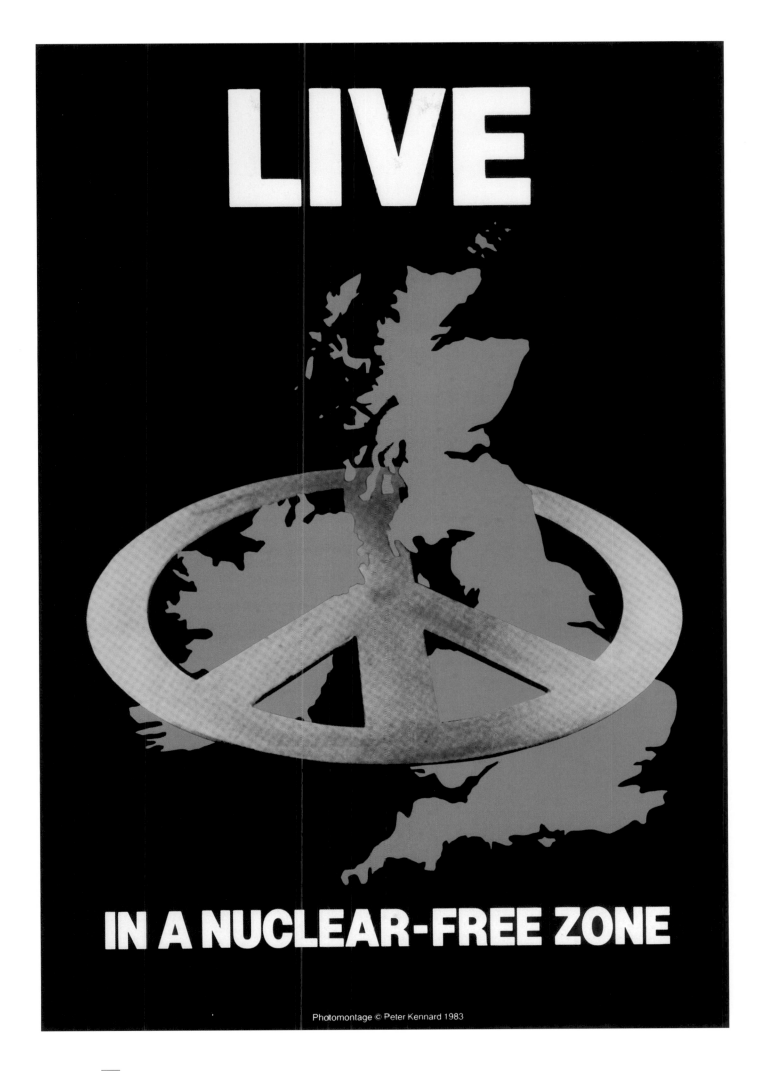

Photomontage © Peter Kennard 1983

Peter Kennard 298 **Live in a nuclear-free zone** 1983
UK

STOP NUCLEAR SUICIDE CAMPAIGN FOR NUCLEAR DISARMAMENT 2 CARTHUSIAN ST LONDON EC1

F. H. K. Henrion 299 **Stop nuclear suicide** 1963
UK

Robert Ross 300 **Eat me** 1967
USA

Alexander Schiel 301 **The NATO way – missile launch! STOP** c.1983
German Democratic Republic

ANTIIMPERIALISTISCHE SOLIDARITÄT

NO CRUISE MISSILES HERE

THE LABOUR PARTY

P/014/80 Published by the Labour Party, 150 Walworth Road, London, SE17 1JT
and printed by Victoria House Printing Company, 26 Cowcross Street, London, EC2

Peter Kennard 302 **No cruise missiles here** 1980
UK

Gerhard Voigt 303 **Anti-Imperialist solidarity** 1981
German Democratic Republic

305 Above

Both Jack Rickard and Jerry DeFuccio worked for the celebrated satirical magazine *MAD*.

A GREAT PLACE FOR HAMBURGERS BUT WHO'D WANT TO LIVE THERE!

Issued by The Great American Disaster Restaurant 335 Fulham Road London SW10

Alan Aldridge **306** **A great place for hamburgers but who'd want to live there!** 1971
UK

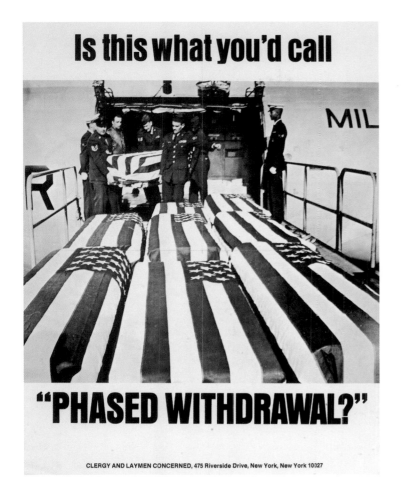

309 Above right

Ungerer's poster is an ironic reworking of popular American images of the folk hero Paul Revere and his nocturnal ride warning of the advance of British forces and heralding the start of the American Revolutionary War in 1775. In so doing Ungerer likens the US Army in Vietnam to the British Army in America.

Unknown **308** Is this what you'd call 'phased withdrawal?' c.1968
USA

Tomi Ungerer **309** The Americans are coming 1967
USA

Unknown 310 **Smash Unionist Junta Stormont** c.1972
Northern Ireland

Unknown 311 **Judge, jury and executioner. Don't fraternise** c.1972
Northern Ireland

310

The influence of the Protestant Orange Order over the Northern Ireland parliament was suspended in 1972 and is shown being smashed with the red fist of the revolutionary socialism advocated by the People's Democracy.

311 Above right

This poster was published by the People's Democracy, a political organization that supported the campaign for civil rights for Northern Ireland's Catholic minority, and campaigned for the establishment of a socialist republic for all of Ireland.

312 Right

At a Northern Ireland Civil Rights Association anti-internment march in Derry on 30 January 1972, thirteen unarmed demonstrators were shot dead by British troops in what became known as 'Bloody Sunday'.

313 Opposite page

Pictured next to Karl Marx, James Connolly was a founder member of the Irish Socialist Republican Party and executed in 1916. This poster refers to the British refusal to accept political status for IRA prisoners.

Unknown 312 **End internment. Aug. 9, 1971–Aug. 9, 1972. And still there** 1972
Northern Ireland

WORKERS OF THE WORLD UNITE

FREE ALL
IRISH POLITICAL PRISONERS

Unknown **313** **Workers of the world unite. Free all Irish political prisoners** c.1970
Northern Ireland

THE COLD WAR AND THE NEW WORLD ORDER

241

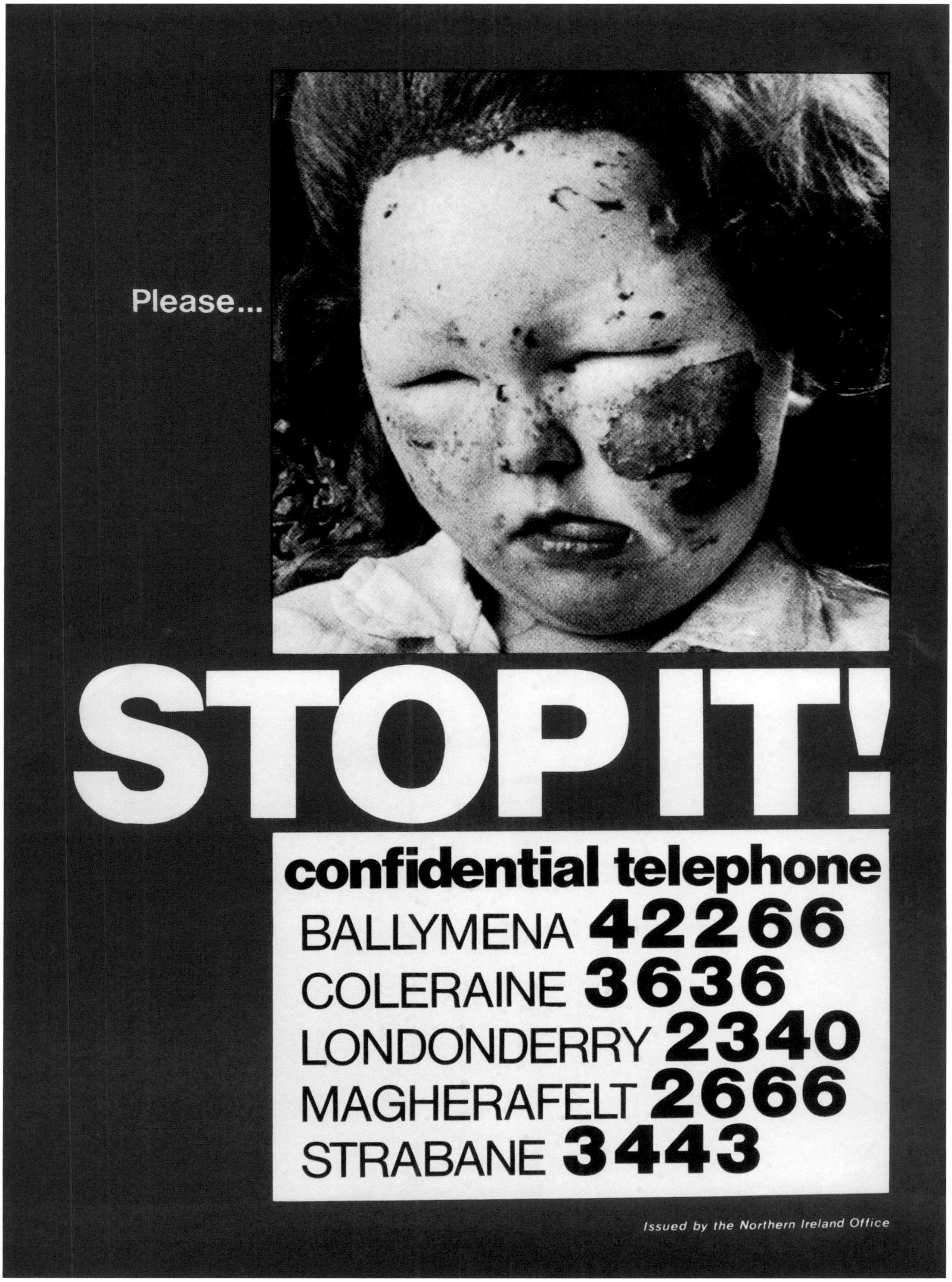

Please...
STOP IT!
confidential telephone
BALLYMENA 42266
COLERAINE 3636
LONDONDERRY 2340
MAGHERAFELT 2666
STRABANE 3443
Issued by the Northern Ireland Office

Unknown 314 **Stop it!** c.1972
Northern Ireland

315 Page 243

Yesh Gvul ('There is a limit') is an Israeli peace group that campaigns against the occupation of Palestinian territories by backing soldiers who refuse duties of a repressive or aggressive nature.

Trio Sarajevo (Dalida Hadİilhalilovic, Bojan Hadİilhalilovic and Leila Hatt) **316** **Enjoy Sarajevo** 1992–93
Bosnia Herzegovina

UNITED COLORS OF NETANYAHU.

iRaq

10,000 Iraqis killed. 773 US soldiers dead.

317 Above

David Tartakover sees himself as 'a seismographer of social and political phenomena in Israel.' This poster won a bronze medal in 2000 at the 17th International Poster Biennial, Warsaw, and questions the role of Benjamin Netanyahu, Israel's former Prime Minister.

318 Right

This poster was created by a New York artist's collective whose members prefer anonymity. Working under the name Copper Greene (the code name used by the Pentagon to describe its programme of prisoner abuse in Iraq) these artists turned Apple's iPod ad campaign on its head by featuring the infamous image of an Iraqi prisoner tortured by American jailers at Abu Ghraib prison in Iraq.

David Tartakover (photograph by David Karp) **317** **United Colors of Netanyahu** 1998
Israel

Copper Greene **318** **iRaq. 10,000 Iraqis killed. 773 US soldiers dead** 2004
USA

THE COLD WAR AND THE NEW WORLD ORDER

245

ARTISTSAGAINSTTHEWAR@hotmail.com

LEON KUHN © 2003

"MAD DOGS AND ENGLISHMEN..."

Leon Kuhn **319 Mad dogs and Englishmen** 2003
UK

Karmarama (Naresh Ramchandani and Dave Buonaguidi) 320 **Make tea not war** 2004
UK

NEW WORLD ORDER

248   Ralph Steadman 321 **Government health warning. War kills** 2003
UK

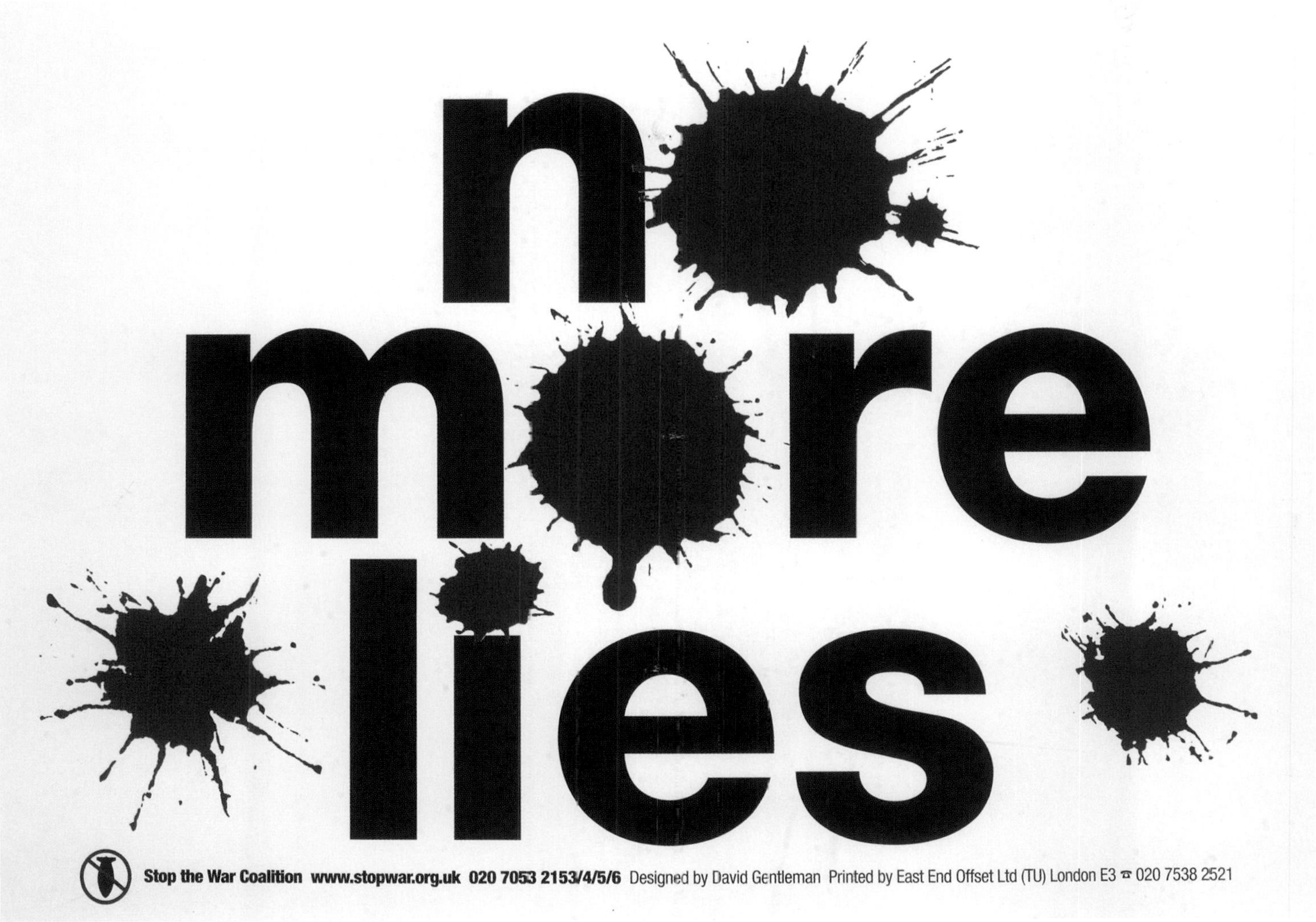

no more lies
Stop the War Coalition www.stopwar.org.uk 020 7053 2153/4/5/6 Designed by David Gentleman Printed by East End Offset Ltd (TU) London E3 ☎ 020 7538 2521

David Gentleman 322 **No more lies** 2004
UK

Bibliography

Ades, D., *The 20th Century Poster. Design of the Avant-Garde*, New York, 1984

Adorno, T. and Horkheimer, M., *Dialectic of Enlightenment*, London, 1979

Art and Industry, London [Vol. 26 (1939) – Vol. 39 (1945)], 1939–45

ARTnews, The first complete survey of war posters [vol. 41], August–September, 1942

Arvidson, C. and Blomqvist, L. E. (eds), *Symbols of Power, The Aesthetics of Political Legitimation in the Soviet Union and Eastern Europe*, Stockholm, 1987

Aulich, J. and Sylvestrova, M., *Political Posters in Central and Eastern Europe, 1945–95*, Manchester, 1999

Aulich, J. and Hewitt, J., *Seduction or Instruction? First World War Posters in Britain and Europe*, Manchester, 2007

Aulich, J. and Wilcox, T. (eds), *Europe without Walls. Art, Posters and Revolution, 1989–93*, Manchester, 1993

Aynsley, J., *Graphic Design in Germany 1890–1945*, London, 2000

Baburina, N., *Russia 20th Century. History of the Country in Poster*, Moscow, 1993

Baburina, N., *The Soviet Political Poster, 1917–1980*, Harmondsworth, 1985

Barnicoat, J., *Private Pursuits and Public Problems. An Exhibition of the Philip Granville Poster Collection*, London, 1993

Barson, M. and Heller, S., *Red Scared! The Commie Menace in Propaganda and Popular Culture*, San Francisco, 2001

Bartelt, D. et al, *Both Sides of Peace. Israeli and Palestinian Political Poster Art*, Seattle, 1996

Bartlett, F. C., *Political Propaganda*, Cambridge, 1940

Beaverbrook, Lord, *The Spirit of the Soviet Union. Anti-Nazi cartoons and Posters*, London, 1942

Becker, J., *The Great War and the French People*, Leamington Spa, 1985

Benjamin, W., *Selected Writings, Vols 1–4*, Harvard, 1996–2003

Bernays, E. L., *Propaganda*, New York, 1928

Bernays, E. L. (ed.), *The Engineering of Consent*, Norman, 1955

Bestley, R. and Noble, I., *International Poster Design*, Mies, 2002

Bird, W. L. and Rubenstein, H. R., *Design for Victory. World War II Posters on the American Home Front*, New York, 1998

Bogart, M. H., *Artists, Advertising and the Borders of Art*, Chicago and London, 1995

Bohrmann, H., *Politische Plakate*, Dortmund, 1987

Borkan, G. A., *World War I Posters*, Atglen PA, 2002

Blum, J. M., *V was for Victory. Politics and American Culture during World War II*, San Diego, New York and London, 1976

Boehm, E., *Behind Enemy Lines. WWII Allied/Axis Propaganda*, Secaucus, NJ, 1989

Bonnell, V., *Iconography of Power. Soviet Political Posters under Lenin and Stalin*, Berkeley, Los Angeles and London, 1997

Bradley, J. and Powers, R., *Flags of Our Fathers*, London, 2006 (2nd edition)

Cantwell, J. D., *Images of War. British Posters 1939–45*, London, 1989

Chomsky, N., *Necessary Illusions. Thought Control in Democratic Societies*, London, 1989

Clark, B., *The Advertising Smoke Screen*, New York and London, 1944.

Clark, T., *Art and Propaganda in the Twentieth Century*, London, 1997.

COI, *Persuading the People. Government Publicity in the Second World War*, London, 1995

Creel, G., *How we advertised America*, New York and London, 1920

Darracott, J. and Loftus, B., *Second World War Posters*, London, 1972

Devaux, S. (ed.), *La Derniere Guerre vue a travers les Affiches*, Paris, 1978

Doll, M. F. V. (ed.), *The Poster War. Allied Propaganda Art of the First World War*, Alberta, 1993

Ford-Hutchinson, S. and Rothwell, A., *The public's perception of advertising in today's society. Prepared for the Advertising Standards Association*, London, February 2002

Fox, F., *Madison Avenue Goes to War. The Strange Military Career of American Advertising, 1941–45*, Provo, 1975

Frantzen, A. J., *Bloody Good. Chivalry, Sacrifice, and the Great War*, Chicago, 2004

Gallo, M., *The Poster in History*, Feltham, Middlesex, 1975

Gregory, G. H., *Posters of World War II*, New York, 1993

Guerra, A. et al, *Carteles de la Guerra 1936–1939*, Barcelona, 1936

Guttsman, W. L., *Art for the Workers. Ideology and the visual arts in Weimar Germany*, Manchester, New York, 1997

Farkash, A. and Halfi, S. *Revolution or Terror? After the Tragedy of September 11th*, Jaffa, 2002

Finkova, D. and Petrova, S., *The Militant Poster 1936–1985*, Prague, 1986

Habermas, J., *The Structural Transformation of the Public Sphere*, Oxford and Cambridge, 1989

Hagelstein M. V., *Art and Journals on the Political Front*, Florida, 1997

Hardie, M. and Sabin, A. K., *War Posters issued by Belligerent and Neutral Nations 1914–1919*, London, 1920

Haste, C., *Keep the Home Fires Burning. Propaganda in the First World War*, London, 1979

Herman, E. S. and Chomsky, N., *Manufacturing Consent. The Political Economy of the Mass Media*, New York, 1988

Herzstein, R. E., *The War that Hitler Won. Nazi Propaganda*, London, 1979

Higham, C. F., *Scientific Distribution*, London, 1916

Hinz, B., *Art in the Third Reich*, Oxford, 1979

Hillier, B., *Posters*, London, 1969

HKS 13, *hoch die kampf dem, 20 Jahre Plakate autonomer Bewegungen*, Hamburg-Berlin-Gottingen, 1999

Holquin, S., *Creating Spaniards. Culture and National Identity in Republican Spain*, Wisconsin, 2002

Hollis, R., *Graphic Design. A Concise History*, London, revised 2001

Holman, V. and Kelly, D., *France at War on the Twentieth Century*, New York and Oxford, 2000

Holme, C. G., *Art in the USSR*, London and New York, 1935

Honey, M., *Creating Rosie the Riveter. Class, Gender and Propaganda during World War II*, Amherst, 1984

Jackall, R., *Propaganda*, New York, 1995

Jahn, H. F., *Patriotic Culture in Russia during World War I*, Ithaca and London, 1995

Jobling, P. and Crowley, D., *Graphic Design. Reproduction and Representation since 1800*, Manchester and New York, 1996

Judd, D., *Second World War Posters*, London, 1971

Kauffer, M. E., *The Art of the Poster*, London, 1924

Keen, S., *Faces of the Enemy. Reflections of the Hostile Imagination. The Psychology of Enmity*, San Francisco, 1986

Kiaer, C., *Imagine No Possessions: The Socialist Objects of Russian Constructivism*, Cambridge, Mass., 2005

Kimble, J. J., *Mobilizing the Home Front. War Bonds and Domestic Propaganda*, College Station, Texas, 2006

Kundera, M., *The Unbearable Lightness of Being*, London, 1985

Kunzle, D., *Art as a Political Weapon: American Posters of Protest 1966–70*, New York, 1971

Lakoff, G. and Johnson, M., *Metaphors We Live By*, Chicago, 1980

Lambert, R. S., *Propaganda*, London, 1938.

Lasswell, H. D. and Blumenstock, D., *World Revolutionary Propaganda. A Chicago Study*, New York and London, 1939

Le Bon, G., *The Crowd*, London, 1952 (first published in English 1896)

Lippard, L., *Get the Message? A decade of Art for Social Change*, New York, 1984

Lippard, L., *A Different War. Vietnam in Art*, Seattle, 1990

Macpherson, W., *The Psychology of Persuasion*, London, 1920

MacKenzie, A. J., *Propaganda Boom*, London, 1938

Mann, J. H. (ed.), *Carteles Contra una Guerra. Signos por la Paz*, Barcelona, 2003

Marchetti, S., *Affiches 1939–1945. Images d'une certaine France*, Milan, 1982

Margadant, B., *Hoffnung und Wiederstand. Das 20. Jahrhundert im Plakat der internationalen Arbeiter und Friedenbewegung*, Zurich, 1998

Marling, K. A. and Wettenhall, J., *Iwo Jima. Monuments, Memories, and the American Hero*, Cambridge, Massachusetts and London, 1991

Massiczek, A. and Sagl, H., *Zeit und Wand*, Vienna, 1967

McLaine, I., *Ministry of Morale. Home Front Morale and the Ministry of Information in World War II*, London, 1979

McQuiston, L., *Graphic Agitation. Social and Political Graphics since the Sixties*, Phaidon, 1993

McQuiston, L., *Graphic Agitation 2. Social and Political Graphics in the Digital Age*, Phaidon, 2004

Mendelson, J., *Documenting Spain. Artists, Exhibition Culture, and the Modern Nation, 1929–1939*, Pennsylvania, 2005

Mercer, F. A. and Lovat Fraser, G. (eds), *Modern Publicity in War*, London and New York, 1941

Mercer, F. A. and Rosner, C. (eds), *Modern Publicity 1942–48*, London and New York, 1948

Mock, J. R. and Larsen, C., *Words that Won the War. The Story of The Committee on Public Information 1917–1919*, San Francisco, 1984

Nelson, C., *Shouts from the Wall. Posters and Photographs brought home from the Spanish Civil War by American Volunteers*, Waltham, Mass., 1996

Nelson, D., *The Posters that Won the War. The Production, Recruitment and War Bond Posters of WWII*, Osceola, 1991

Nerai, K., *The Contemporary Hungarian Poster*, Budapest Art Gallery, 1985

O'Shaughnessey, N. J., *Politics and Propaganda. Weapons of Mass Seduction*, Manchester, 2004

Outdoor Advertising Association of America, *Outdoor Advertising. The Modern Marketing Force*, Chicago, 1928

Paret, P., Irwin Lewis, B. and Paret, P., *Persuasive Images. Posters of War and Revolution*, Princeton, 1992

Phillippe, R., *Political Graphics: Art as a Weapon*, Oxford, 1982

Ponsonby, A., *Falsehood in War Time: Containing An Assortment of Lies Circulated Throughout The Nations During The Great War*, New York, 1928

Poster Advertising Association, *The Poster War Souvenir Edition*, Chicago, 1920

Povazai, L., *100+1 Years of Hungarian Posters. The History of Hungarian Poster Design 1885–1986*, Budapest, undated

Rawls, W., *Wake Up, America! World War I and the American Poster*, New York, London, Paris, 1998

Reed, T. V., *The Art of Protest. Culture and Activism from the Civil Rights Movement to the Streets of Seattle*, Minnesota, 2005

Rhodes, A., *Propaganda. The Art of Persuasion: World War II an Allied and Axis Visual Record, 1933–1945*, London, Sydney and Melbourne, 1975

Rickards, M., *Posters of Protest and Revolution*, New York, 1970

Rickards, M., *Posters of the First World War*, London, 1968

Roeder, G. H., *The Censored War. American Visual Experience During World War Two*, New Haven and London, 1993

Rose, S. O., *Which People's War? National Identity and Citizenship in Wartime Britain, 1939–1945*, Oxford, 2002

Rosgen, P. (ed.), *Bilder und Macht im 20. Jahrhundert*, Bonn, 2004

Rothschild, D., Lupton, E. and Goldstein, D., *Graphic Design in the Mechanical Age*, New Haven and London, 1998

Russell, B., *Free Thought and Official Propaganda*, Conway Memorial Lecture, London, 1922

Rutherford, P., *Endless Propaganda. The Advertising of Public Goods*, Toronto, 2000

Rutherford, W., *Hitler's propaganda Machine*, London, 1978

Sahlstrom, B., *Political Posters in Ethiopia and Mozambique. Visual Imagery in a Revolutionary Context*, Stockholm, 1990

St Clair, L., *The Story of the Liberty Loans*, Washington, 1919

Samuel, L. R., *Pledging Allegiance. American Identity and the Bond Drive of World War II*, Washington and London, 1997

Sarhandi, D. and Boboc, A., *Evil Doesn't Live Here. Posters from the Bosnian War*, London, 2001

Saunders, M. L. and Taylor, P.M., *British Propaganda during the First World War 1914–1918*, London, 1982

Schnapp, J. T., *Revolutionary Tides. The Art of the Political Poster 1914–1989*, New York, 2005

Schwartz, F. J., *The Werkbund: Design Theory and Mass culture before the First World War*, New Haven and London, 1996

Scott, W. D., *The Theory and Practice of Advertising. A Simple Exposition of The Principles of Psychology In Their Relation to Successful Advertising*, Boston, 1908

Sheldon, C., *A History of Poster Advertising*, London, 1937

Shockel, E., *Das Politische Plakat*. Munich, 1938

Stark, G., *Moderne politische Propaganda*, Munich, 1930

Sylvestrova, M. and Bartel, D., *Art as Activist*, London, 1992

Taylor, P. M., *British Propaganda in the Twentieth Century. Selling Democracy*, Edinburgh, 1999

Teitelbaum, M. and Freiman, L. (eds), *Montage and Modern Life, 1919–1942*, Cambridge, Mass., 1992

The Russian State Library, *The Russian Poster 20th Century Masterpieces*, Moscow, 2000

Theofiles, G., *American Posters of World War I*, New York, undated

Timmers, Margaret (ed.), *The Power of the Poster*, London, 1998

Track 16 Gallery, Center for the Study of Political Graphics, *decade of protest. political posters from the UNITED STATES, VIETNAM, CUBA, 1965–1975*, Santa Monica, California, 1996

Tupitsyn, Margarita, *Glaube, Hoffnung – Anpassung. Sowjeische Bilder 1928–1945*, Oberhausen, 1996

Unknown, *The Poster in the Struggle for Peace, Security and Cooperation*, Moscow, 1985

Unknown, *Russian Poster of World War One*, Moscow, 1992

Viereck, G. S., *Spreading Germs of Hate*, London, 1931

Walsh, J. and Aulich, J., *Vietnam Images. War and Representation*, London, 1989

Weill, A., *The Poster*, London, 1984

Weill, A., *Affiches Politiques et Sociales*, Paris, 1995

Welch, D., *The Third Reich. Politics and Propaganda*, London and New York, 1993

Welch, D., *Germany, Propaganda and Total War, 1914–1918*, New Brunswick, New Jersey and London, 2000

White, S., *The Bolshevik Poster*, New Haven and London, 1998

Winter, J., *Sites of Memory, Sites of Mourning. The Great War in European cultural history*, Cambridge, 1995

Wrede, S., *The Modern Poster*, New York, 1998

Wright, M., *You Back the Attack, We'll Bomb Who We Want*, New York, 2003

Yanker, G., *Prop Art*, New York 1972

Yass, M., *This is your War. Home Front Propaganda in the Second World War*, London, 1983

Zaccaria, D., *Un Combat des Symboles. Un Siecle d'affiches politiques en Europe*, REAGA, 2006

Zeman, Z., *Selling the War: Art and Propaganda in World War II*, London, 1978

Ziff, T. (ed.), *Che Guevara: Revolutionary Icon*, London, 2006

Useful websites

Another Poster For Peace
www.anotherposterforpeace.org

At war with Iraq: the propaganda battles
www.classroomtools.com/iraq_war.htm

The Austrian National Library
www.onb.ac.at/ev/collections/flu/index.htm

Blood for Oil
www.bloodforoil.org

Brandeis University
www.brandeis.edu/overview

Calvin College – German Propaganda Archive
www.calvin.edu/academic/cas/gpa/stark.htm

Campaign on Iraq
www.miniaturegigantic.com

Center for the Study of Political Graphics
www.politicalgraphics.org

Center for Sales, Advertising and Marketing History
http://scriptorium.lib.duke.edu/adaccess/

Etapes
www.etapes.com

The History Cooperative
www.historycooperative.org/journals/whc/1.2/gilbert.html

The History of Advertising Trust
www.hatads.org.uk/collection.htm

Holt Labor Library
www.holtlaborlibrary.org/anti-war.html

The Imperial War Museum
www.iwm.org.uk

Media.studies.ca – Propaganda at War
www.mediastudies.ca/articles/war_propaganda.htm

Micah Wright
http://micahwright.com

The National Archives (UK)
www.nationalarchives.gov.uk/theartofwar

The National Archives (US)
http://www.archives.gov/exhibits/powers_of_persuasion/powers_of_persuasion_intro.html

Protest Posters
www.protestposters.org

Protest posters today and in history
http://maillists.uci.edu/mailman/public/ethnicstudies/2003-February/000075.html

Rene Wanner's Poster Page
www.posterpage.ch/index.html

Robert Opie British nostalgia and advertising memorabilia
www.robertopiecollection.com

Ruavista: Signs of the city
www.ruavista.com/links.htm#enseignes

Second World War Posters
www.ww2poster.co.uk

The Sixties Project
http://lists.village.virginia.edu/sixties/HTML_docs/Exhibits/Track16.html

The Smithsonian American Art Museum
http://americanart.si.edu/collections/exhibits/posters/mainmenu.html

United for peace and justice
www.unitedforpeace.org/article.php?id=592

The Victoria and Albert Museum – Posters
www.vam.ac.uk/nal/guides/posters/index.html

World War II Propaganda, Cartoons, Film, Music and Art
www.teacheroz.com/WWIIpropaganda.htm

Yo! What Happened to Peace? – An exhibition of peace/anti-war/anti-occupation posters
yowhathappenedtopeace.org

Illustration list

Many thanks to Dr Sheelagh Ellwood for her assistance with Spanish Civil War picture research.

Every possible effort has been made to locate and credit copyright holders of the material reproduced in this book. The Imperial War Museum and the publisher apologize for any omissions or errors, which can be corrected in future editions.

Artists dates and names are given where known.

Page 1
August William (Angiet) Hutaf (1879–1942), Send 'em "the slam" from Alabam', 1917, Air Nitrates Corporation, National Printing and Engraving Co., New York, Chicago and St Louis [IWM PST 17360]

Page 2
Unknown, Which ought you to wear?, 1914, Publicity Department, Central London Recruiting Depot, Whitehall, Sir Joseph Causton and Sons Ltd, London [IWM PST 7664]

Page 5
H. Devitt Welsh (1888–1942), They give their lives. Do you lend your savings?, c.1918, United States Treasury and Committee on Public Information, Division of Pictorial Publicity [IWM PST 17290]

Gerald Spencer Pryse (1882–1956), Belgian Red Cross Fund, 1915, Belgian Red Cross Fund, Johnson, Riddle and Co. Ltd, London [IWM PST 0361]

Ferdy Horrmeyer (1890–1960), Wählt Sozialistisch (Vote Socialist), 1919, A. Molling & Co., Hanover and Berlin [IWM PST 6304]

John Atherton (1900–52), A careless word ... another cross, 1943, Office of War Information, Washington DC, US Government Printing Office [IWM PST 0622]

Jamie Reid (1947–), Peace is tough, 2003, Stop the War Coalition [IWM PST 8857]

1: Peter Kennard (1949–), Untitled (Poster Number 1, Stop the War Coalition), 2003. Courtesy the artist [IWM PST 8854]

2: The Mayor of Westminster makes a public appeal for war bonds in Trafalgar Square, London, 1917 [IWM Photograph Archive Q54094]

3: Maurice Neumont (1868–1930), On ne passe pas! (They shall not pass!), 1918, Union des Grandes Associations Françaises, Devambez Imprimerie, Paris [IWM PST 3950]

4: Unknown, Terrorists? You have seen them. Are you going to tell the authorities about them?, 2003, MND [SE] (Multinational Division South East) and Ministry of Defence, Iraq [IWM PST 8898]

5: Oliviero Toscani (b 1942), United Colors of Benetton, 1993, Occhipinti i Sisar Spa. Accepted by HM Government in Lieu of Inheritance Tax and allocated to the Imperial War Museum, 2007 [IWM PST 9035 1-2]

6: A boy peeling a poster featuring a portrait of President Allawi from a wall in Baghdad, Iraq, 2005. Ali Yussef/AFP/Getty Images

7: A poster protesting against the UK government's involvement in Iraq outside the Palace of Westminster in London, designed by David Gentleman on behalf of the Stop the War Coalition, 2003. Photo Moramay Herrera Kuri

8: Mark Wallinger's 'State Britain' in Tate Britain, London, 2007. © Tate, London 2007

9: Brian Haw, view of protest, Parliament Square, London, 2006. Photo Terry Dennett/www.parliament-square.org.uk

10: Chris Savido's (1981–) 'Bush Monkeys' portrait of US President George W. Bush, New York, 2004. Stan Honda/AFP/Getty Images

11: J. Allen St John (1872–1957), Blot it out with liberty bonds, 1917, Brett Litho Co., New York [IWM PST 17244]

12: Adolf Uzarski (1885–1970), Wie eine bombe (Like a bomb), 1918, A. Bagel, Düsseldorf [IWM PST 7379]

13: Ellsworth Young (1866–1952), Remember Belgium, 1918, US Printing and Lithographic Co. [IWM PST 0303]

14: Trio Sarajevo (Dalida HadĨilhalilovic, Bojan HadĨilhalilovic and Leila Hatt), Sarajevo Olympics, 1994. Courtesy the artists [IWM PST 8598]

15: Pat Keely (?–1970), Indie moet vrij! (The Indies shall be freed!), 1944, HMSO for the Netherlands Government in exile, James Haworth & Brother Ltd, London [IWM PST 0120]

16: Alfred Leete (1882–1933), Britons join your country's army!, 1914, Victoria House Printing Co. Ltd, London [IWM PST 2734]

17: Achille Luciano Mauzan (1883–1952), Fate tutti il vostro dovere! (Do your whole duty), 1917, Credito Italiano, G. Ricordi e Co., Milano. © ADAGP, Paris and DACS, London 2007 [IWM PST 6595]

18: James Montgomery Flagg (1877–1960), I want you for US army, 1917, Leslie Judge, New York [IWM PST 2747]

19: Personality Posters (after James Montgomery Flagg), I want you for US army, c.1972, T. J. Press Ltd, London [IWM PST 2524]

20: Unknown, More production, 1942, War Production Board, Washington DC, US Government Printing Office [IWM PST 0037]

21: Unknown, Per ogni bomba nel 1939, trenta bombe nel 1943 (For every bomb in 1939, thirty bombs in 1943), 1943, La Parola delle Nazione Unite [IWM PST 8646]

22: David G. Bragin (1944–), Under Nixon 3 million tons of bombs dropped on Indochina, 1972, New York. Courtesy David G. Bragin [IWM PST 8276]

23: Ben Shahn (1898–1969), This is Nazi brutality, 1942, United States Office of War Information, US Government Printing Office [IWM PST 0093]

24: Unknown, End the torture, 2004, Stop the War Coalition, East End Offset Ltd. (TU), London. Courtesy Stop the War Coalition [IWM PST 8807]

25: Fernando C. Amorsolo (1892–1972), Sus bonos de la libertad ayudaran a dar fin con esto (Your liberty bond will help stop this), c.1917–18, Bureau of Printing, Manila [IWM PST 17260]

26: David Wilson (1873–1935), How the Hun hates!, 1915–18, The Dangerfield Printing Co. Ltd, London [IWM PST 13551]

27: Theo Matejko (1893–1946), Katyn, le paradis sous terre (Katyn, paradise below ground), 1943 [IWM PST 9274]

28: United States Holocaust Memorial Museum Committee on Conscience (photograph by Michael Wadleigh), Sexual violence is a tool of genocide, 2006. United States Holocaust Memorial Museum, Washington [IWM PST 9319]

29: Fraser Dougherty, Jon Hendricks and Irving Petlin (photograph by Ronald Haeberle), Q: And babies? A: And babies, 1969, The Art Workers' Coalition, New York [IWM PST 2538]

30: Theo Matejko (1893–1946), Les femmes et les enfants d'Europe accusent! (The women and children of Europe accuse!), 1940 [IWM PST 2804]

31: Attributed to Augusto (photograph by Robert Capa), What are you doing to prevent this?, 1937, Ministerio de Propaganda, Madrid [IWM PST 8660]

32: Viktor Koretsky (1909–98), Red Army soldier, save us!, 1943, Iskusstvo, Moscow [IWM PST 6136]

33: David Tartakover (1944–), Stop the killing of children, 1991, *Betzelem*, Israel. Courtesy the artist [IWM PST 8948]

34: Unknown, Kein blut für öl! Hände weg vom Irak! (No blood for oil! Hands off Iraq!), 2003, Internationale Frauenliga für Frieden und Freiheit, Deutscher Friedensrat, Friedensglockengesellschaft Berlin e. V, Attac Jugend Berlin, Attac Frauennetz, WOF! Plannungsgemeinschaft, Demokratische Linke [IWM PST 8864]

35: Unknown, Maneater, 1941–42, Ministry of Information, Stafford and Co. Ltd, Netherfield, Nottingham [IWM PST 0176]

36: Koehler (1913–2000) and Ancona (1912–), Ecco il nemico (This is the enemy), 1942, Artists for Victory Association, the Lithographers' National Association, the Council for Democracy, Museum of Modern Art, New York, R. Hoe & Co. Ltd. Courtesy R. Hoe & Co. Inc. [IWM PST 0796]

37: Norman Alfred William Lindsay (1879–1969), ?, 1918, Government of the Commonwealth of Australia, C. Steele and Co. [IWM PST 3242]

38: Rieuiey, Protest der deutschen frauen gegen die farbige besatzung am Rhein (German women's protest against the coloured occupation troops on the Rhine), 1923–24, Plakatkunstanstalt Dinse und Eckert, Berlin [IWM PST 8515]

39: Unknown, Prevent forest fires! Careless matches aid the Axis, 1942, US Department of Agriculture, Forest Service, US Government Printing Office [IWM PST 17442]

40: G. Bartoletti, Pax Britannica, 1943, Studio Tecnico Editoriale Italiano, Roma Cronache, N. Moneta, Milano [IWM PST 5761]

41: Pere Català Pic (Roca) (c.1889–c.1971), Aixafem el Feixisme (Smash Fascism), 1936, La Comissaria de Propaganda de la Generalitat de Catalunya [IWM PST 8479]

42: F. H. K. Henrion (1914–90), Untitled, 1944, US Office of War Information. Courtesy the Estate of F. H. K. Henrion [IWM PST 4006]

43: Otto Lehmann (1865–?), Stützt unsre feldgrauen – zereisst Englands macht (Help our men in uniform break England's power), 1917, Wilhelm Eisfeller Graphische Kunstanstalt, Köln [IWM PST 6176]

44: Guy Lipscombe (1881–1952), It's our flag. Fight for it. Work for it, 1915, Parliamentary Recruiting Committee, Henry Jenkinson Ltd, Kirkstall, Leeds [IWM PST 5071]

45: A girl at work with ladder and paste carries on her father's appointment of Official Bill Poster and Town Crier, Thetford [IWM Photograph Archive, Q 31028]

46: A. Grebel, Ohé les Copains! (Hey Lads!), 1915, Augendre, Atelier Grebel, Paris [IWM PST 12911]

47: Mihály Biró (1886–1948), Pesti napló (Pest diary), 1917, Radó, Budapest [IWM PST 5957]

48: Jocheim, Die Deutsche kriegspfanne. Das kriegserinnerungszeichen der Deutschen hausfrau (The German war pan. The war memorial of the German housewife), 1917–18, Gerstung, Offenbach [IWM PST 7594]

49: Unknown, Zeichnet siebente kriegs-Anleihe (Subscribe to the seventh war loan), 1917, J. Weiner, Wien [IWM PST 10613]

50: Alfred Offner (1879–c.1937), Zeichnet siebente kriegsanleihe (Subscribe to the seventh war loan), 1917, Wiener Kommerzial Bank, J. Weiner, Wien [IWM PST 4823]

51: Unknown, You are no exception. Join now, 1914, Central Recruiting Committee, No.2 Military Division, Toronto, Stone Ltd,. Archives of Ontario, War Posters [C233-2-1-0-199] [IWM PST 12435]

52: Ernest Linzell, Hold up your end, 1918, Red Cross Society, Waterlow Bros and Layton Ltd, London [IWM PST 10837]

53: Richard Klein (1890–1967), Opfertag (Flag day), 1917, Deutsches Rotes Kreuz (German Red Cross), Dr C. Wolf und Sohn, München [IWM PST 7613]

54: Unknown (photograph by Sampson Tchernoff), Countryless!, 1916–17, Serbian Relief Fund [IWM PST 10956]

55: York Railway Station, UK, 1915 [IWM Photograph Archive, Q 80627]

56: National War Bonds and Corps Cinema advertisements in Hinges, France, 1918 [IWM Photograph Archive, Q 6538]

57: S. E. M. (Georges Goursat) (1863–1934), Pour le triomphe souscrivez à l'emprunt national (For victory subscribe to the national loan), 1916, Banque Nationale de Credit, Devambez Impremerie [IWM PST 4345]

58: R. H. Porteous, Women! Help America's sons win the war. Buy US Government bonds 2nd liberty loan, 1917, United States Treasury, Edwards & Deutsch Litho Co., Chicago [IWM PST 0231]

59: James Montgomery Flagg (1877–1960), Together we win, 1918, United States Shipping Board, Emergency Fleet Corporation, W. F. Powers Litho Co., New York [IWM PST 17359]

60: Walter Ditz (1888–1925), Opfertag – glüh heilge flamme glüh, glüh und erlösche nie fürs vaterland (Flag day. Burn sacred flame burn. Burn and never cease to burn for the Fatherland), 1918, Dr C. Wolf und Sohn, München [IWM PST 11317]

61: Albert Bailey, Comradeship! Territorials, 1920, Territorial Army, Sprague & Co. Ltd [IWM PST 4891]

62: Ludwig Hohlwein (1874–1949), Bulgarenheld (Bulgarian Hero cigarettes), 1914–18, Zigarettenfabrik Menes, Wiesbaden, Fritz Maison, München. © DACS 2007 [IWM PST 5979]

63: Bert Thomas (1883–1966), 'Arf a 'mo' Kaiser!, 1914, The Weekly Dispatch Tobacco Fund, Johnson Signs Ltd, London [IWM PST 10799]

64: Frank Dadd (1852–1929), Keep on sending me OXO, 1914, OXO Ltd, London. By permission of Premier Grocery Products Limited [IWM PST 10805]

65: Unknown, Only me and DUNLOPS left, 1914, Dunlop, Hancock and Corfield Ltd Courtesy Goodyear Dunlop Tyres UK Limited [IWM PST 13686]

66: Hans Lindenstaedt (1874–?), Biocitin, 1915–18, Reklamekunst Hans Lindenstaedt, Charlottenburg 5, Berlin [IWM PST 13038]

67: Unknown, Newcao – déjeuner nutritif par excellence (Newcao: nutritious breakfast par excellence), 1917–18, Gros Etablissements Louis Michel, Ogé, Paris [IWM PST 12904]

68: Georges Dola (1872–1950), Ciné-Concert des Alliés (Film concert for the Allies), 1918, 'Novelty' Theatre Paris, Atelier Delattre et Cie, Paris [IWM PST 12643]

69: Bruce Bairnsfather (1888–1959), The Johnson 'Ole, 1916, London Hippodrome, John Waddington Ltd, London and Leeds. Courtesy Tonie and Valmai Holt [IWM PST 3943]

70: Henri Montassier (1880–1946), L'Heure a découvert la machine à finir la guerre (L'Heure has discovered the machine to end the war), 1917, Atelier Charles Didier, Paris [IWM PST 2702]

71: Hans Rudi Erdt (1883–1918), Bei unseren blaujacken (With our boys in blue), 1917, Königliche Bild und Filmamt (Bufa), Hollerbaum und Schmidt, Berlin [IWM PST 7229]

72: S. L. Satori, Uránia – u hajók elöre! (The U-Boats are out!), 1917, Magyar-Osztrák Filmipari Vallalat (Hungarian-Austrian Moving Picture Company), Seidner Plakát és Cimkegyár, Budapest [IWM PST 5958]

73: Jules Abel Faivre (1867–1945), Pour la France versez votre or (Pour forth your gold for France), 1915, Société des Amis des Artistes, Devambez Imprimerie, Paris. © ADAGP, Paris and DACS, London 2007 [IWM PST 12865]

74: Béla Moldován (1895–1967), Jegyezzetek hadikölcsönt (Subscribe to the war loan), 1918, Kunossy Muintézet, Budapest [IWM PST 10577]

75: T. Martin Jones, Buy war loan bonds, 1918, The Times Press, Bombay [IWM PST 13116]

76: D. D. P., Lend your five shillings to your country and crush the Germans, 1915, Parliamentary War Savings Committee, David

Allen and Sons Ltd, 17 Leicester Street, London, W. Belfast, Harrow, Liverpool, Glasgow, Dublin [IWM PST 10063]

77: Unknown, Turn your silver into bullets at the Post Office, 1915, Parliamentary War Savings Committee, Sir Joseph Causton and Sons Ltd [IWM PST 10168]

78: Julius Gipkens (1883–?), DELKA – Deutsche Luftkriegsbeute Asstellung (DELKA – German Air-War Trophies Exhibition), 1917, Delka, Hollerbaum und Schmidt, Berlin [IWM PST 0508]

79: Julius Gipkens (1883–?), Fischer, schafft tran heran! Fangt tümmler u. seehunde! (Fishermen, bring train oil! Catch porpoises and seals!) 1917–18, Kriegsausschuss für Oele und Fette (War Committee for Oils and Fats), Hollerbaum und Schmidt, Berlin [IWM PST 7590]

80: Lucien Bernhard (1883–1972), Achte kriegsanleihe (Eighth war loan), 1918, Hollerbaum und Schmidt, Berlin. © DACS 2007 [IWM PST 10570]

81: Euringer, Bürger Cölns. Sechste kriegsanleihe (Citizens of Cologne. Sixth war loan), 1917, Wilhelm Eisfeller Graphische Kunstanstalt, Köln [IWM PST 0493]

82: Julius Klinger (1876–1942), Achte kriegsanleihe (Eighth war loan), 1918, J. Weiner, Wien [IWM PST 5944]

83: Emil Ranzenhofer (1864–1930), Zeichnet achte kriegsanleihe! (Subscribe to the eighth war loan), 1918, J. Weiner, Wien [IWM PST 2659]

84: Unknown, Buy war bonds now, 1918, National War Savings Committee, The Dangerfield Printing Co. Ltd, London [IWM PST 10440]

85: Unknown, Buy your war bonds now!, 1918, National War Savings Committee, The Dangerfield Printing Co. Ltd, London [IWM PST 10443]

86: After C. R. W. Nevinson, Now, back the bayonets, 1918, National War Savings Committee, The Dangerfield Printing Co. Ltd, London [IWM PST 8167]

87: Unknown, Eat less bread, 1917, Ministry of Food, Hazell, Watson and Viney Ltd, London [IWM PST 6564]

88: John E. Sheridan (1880–1948), Food is ammunition – don't waste it, 1918, United States Food Administration, Heywood, Strasser & Voigt Litho Co., New York [IWM PST 3934]

89: G. Douanne (c.1900–?), Soignons la basse-Cour (Let's look after the farmyard), c.1916, Union Française Comité National de Prévoyance et d'Economies [IWM PST 4735]

90: Unknown, "Springbok" Continental Tour, 1918, South Africa [IWM PST 12334]

91: Unknown, Lend your strong right arm to your country. Enlist now, 1914, Parliamentary Recruiting Committee, H. and C. Graham Ltd, Camberwell, London [IWM PST 11459]

92: Unknown, The key to the situation, are you helping to turn it?, 1915, Parliamentary Recruiting Committee, Seargeant Brothers Ltd, London and Abergavenny [IWM PST 5056]

93: Unknown, Come & join this happy throng off to the front, c.1915–16, HMSO, James Walker (Dublin) Ltd, Dublin and London [IWM PST 13604]

94: Unknown, Step into your place, 1915, Parliamentary Recruiting Committee, David Allen & Sons Ltd, Harrow, Middlesex [IWM PST 0318]

95: Unknown, Come lad slip across and help, 1915, Parliamentary Recruiting Committee, David Allen and Sons Ltd, Harrow, Middlesex [IWM PST 5070]

96: Unknown, The Navy wants men, 1917, Royal Naval Canadian Volunteer Reserve, The Mortimer Co. Ltd, Ottawa, Montreal, Toronto. Archives of Ontario, War Posters [C233-2-0-4-200] [IWM PST 12451]

97: Charles Stafford Duncan (1892–1952), It takes a man to fill it. Join the Navy, 1917, United States Navy, Schmidt Litho, San Francisco [IWM PST 17220]

98: August William (Angiet) Hutaf (1879–1942), Treat 'em rough! Join the tanks, 1918, United States Tank Corps, National Printing and Engraving Co., Chicago, New York, St Louis [IWM PST 2722]

99: Howard Chandler Christy (1873–1952), Gee!! I wish I were a man, I'd join the Navy, 1917, United States Navy [IWM PST 0246]

100: Richard Fayerweather Babcock (1887–1954), Join the Navy. The service for fighting men, 1917, United States Navy [IWM PST 17189]

101: Savile Lumley (1876–c.1950), Daddy, what did YOU do in the Great War?, 1915, Parliamentary Recruiting Committee, Johnson, Riddle and Co. Ltd, Penge, London [IWM PST 0311]

102: E. V. Kealey, Women of Britain say – "Go!", 1915, Parliamentary Recruiting Committee, Hill, Siffken and Co, Ltd, London [IWM PST 2763]

103: James Montgomery Flagg (1877–1960), Boys and girls! You can help your Uncle Sam win the war, 1917, United States Treasury, American Lithographic Co., New York [IWM PST 17289]

104: Auguste Leroux (1871–1954), Souscrivez pour la France qui comfort! Pour celle qui chaque jour grandit (Subscribe for France who fights! For the girl growing up every day), 1917, Imprimerie Joseph Charles, Paris [IWM PST 10498]

105: Joseph Earnest Sampson (1887–1946), Oh please do! Daddy. Buy me a victory bond, 1917, Canada. Archives of Ontario, War Posters [C233-2-1-0-294] [IWM PST 12362]

106: Unknown, We're both needed to serve the guns!, 1915, Parliamentary Recruiting Committee, Chorley and Pickersgill Ltd, Leeds and London [IWM PST 5112]

107: Welsh, Put the Hun on iron rations. 1914–18, Geo Cohen Sons & Co., London [IWM DPB 4217]

108: Walter Whitehead (1874–1956), Stand by the boys in the trenches. Mine more coal, 1918, United States Fuel Administration, Edwards and Deutsch Litho Co., Chicago [IWM PST 17372]

109: Unknown, Elles servent la France. Tout le monde peut servir (They are serving France. Everyone can Serve), 1918, Canadian Victory Loan. Archives of Ontario, War Posters [C233-2-1-0-21b] [IWM PST 12866]

110: B. Chavannaz, Vous aussi faites votre devoir: avec toutes vos ressources (You too are doing your duty: with all your resources subscribe to the war loan), 1918, Crédit Commercial de France, Imprimerie Crété, Paris [IWM PST 3966]

111: Unknown, Don't waste bread! Save two slices every day and Defeat the 'U' Boat, 1917, Ministry of Food, Clarke and Sherwell Ltd, London [IWM PST 13354]

112: Frank Brangwyn (1867–1956), Put strength in the final blow. Buy war bonds, 1918, National War Savings Committee, The Avenue Press (L. Upcott Gill and Son Ltd), Drury Lane, London [IWM PST 5819]

113: Jules Abel Faivre (1867–1945), On les aura! (Let's get them!), 1916, Devambez Imprimerie, Paris. © ADAGP, Paris and DACS, London 2007 [IWM PST 10480]

114: Norman Alfred William Lindsay (1879–1969), The last call, 1918, Government of the Commonwealth of Australia, W. E. Smith Ltd, Sydney [IWM PST 12204]

115: Walter Whitehead (1874–1956), Come on! Buy more liberty bonds, 1918, United States Treasury, Ketterlinus, Philadelphia [IWM PST 0273]

116: Charles Dominique Fouqueray (c.1871–1956), Journée de l'Armée d'Afrique et des Troupes Coloniales (African Army and Colonial Troops day), 1917, L'Office de l'Algerie, I. Lapina Imprimerie, Paris. © ADAGP, Paris and DACS, London 2007 [IWM PST 11182]

117: M. Kivatizky (1873–1943), J'ai une perm' vous voyez, j'viens souscrivez à l'emprunt! (I'm on leave, you see. I'm coming to subscribe to the loan!), 1917, La Platinogravure, Montrouge [IWM PST 10515]

118: Théophile Alexandre Steinlen (1859–1923), Journée Serbe (Serbia day), 1916, Editions 'La Guerre', Paris, I. Lapina Imprimerie, Paris [IWM PST 11081]

119: Lina von Schauroth (1875–1970), Kaiser und volksdank für heer und flotte (Imperial and popular charity fund for the Army and the Navy), 1917, Kaiser und Volksdank für Heer und Flotte, Kunstanstalt Wüsten und Co., Frankfurt [IWM PST 0462]

120: Fritz Erler (1868–1940), Helft uns siegen! (Help us win!), 1917, Hollerbaum und Schmidt, Berlin [IWM PST 0444]

121: Bert Thomas (1883–1966), "Fag" Day, 1917, The Smoke Fund, Witherby and Co. [IWM PST 0415]

122: Ludwig Hohlwein (1874–1949), Ludendorff-spende für kriegsbeschädigte (The Ludendorff appeal for the war-disabled), 1918, Deutsches Rotes Kreuz (German Red Cross), Kunstanstalt Kornsand und Co., Frankfurt. © DACS 2007 [IWM PST 7751]

123: Theo Matejko (1893–1946), Kinder in not! (Children in need!), 1914–18, Deutsche Kinder Volkssammlung [IWM PST 11314]

124: W. B. King, Lest they perish, 1914–18, American Committee for Relief in the Near East, Conwell Graphic Companies, New York [IWM PST 17347]

125: Lucy Elizabeth Kemp Welch (1869–1958), Remember Scarborough! Enlist now, 1915, Parliamentary Recruiting Committee, David Allen and Sons Ltd, Harrow, Middlesex [IWM PST 5109]

126: Unknown, Britain needs you at once, 1915, Parliamentary Recruiting Committee, Spottiswoode and Co. Ltd [IWM PST 0408]

127: Bert Thomas (1883–1966), Joan of Arc saved France. Women of Britain save your country. Buy war savings certificates, 1915, National War Savings Committee, M. and C. Graham Ltd, London [IWM PST 10296]

128: S. T. C. Weeks, Women! Who need skilled jobs ask for free training, 1919, Ministry of Labour, Hill, Siffken and Co. Ltd, London [IWM PST 5475]

129: Frank Lucien Nicolet (1887–?), "If ye break faith – we shall not sleep", 1918, Canada. Archives of Ontario, War Posters [C233-2-1-0-16a] [IWM PST 12361]

130: Unknown, Keep all Canadians busy. Buy 1918 victory bonds, 1918, Canada. Archives of Ontario, War Posters [C233-2-1-0-65] [IWM PST 12400]

131: Jules Abel Faivre (1867–1945), Souscrivez au quatriéme emprunt national (Subscribe to the fourth national loan), 1918, Crédit Lyonnais, Devambez Imprimerie, Paris. © ADAGP, Paris and DACS, London 2007 [IWM PST 4399]

132: Georges Dorival (1879–1968), Après les foyers du soldat, les foyers du civil (After hostels for soldiers, hostels for civilians), 1919, Société des Foyers de l'Union Franco-Americaine and YMCA, Coquemer Imprimerie, Paris. © ADAGP, Paris and DACS, London 2007 [IWM PST 5273]

133: Lucien Jonas (1880–1947), Emprunt National, souscrivez (National loan, subscribe), 1919, Banque L. Dupont et Compagnie, Devambez Imprimerie, Paris. Courtesy the Estate of Lucien Jonas, [IWM PST 6289]

134: Georges Scott (1873–1942), Pour le drapeau! Pour la victoire! (For the flag! For victory!), 1917, Banque Nationale de Crédit, Devambez Imprimerie, Paris [IWM PST 4400]

135: Alfonse Lelong, Banque Privée (Banque Privée. Subscribe to the reconstruction loan), 1919–20, Banque Privée, Imprimerie Joseph Charles, Paris [IWM PST 10736]

136: Gerrit A. Beneker (1882–1934), Sure! We'll finish the job. Victory liberty loan, 1918, United States Treasury, Edwards & Deutsch Litho Co., Chicago [IWM PST 17303]

137: Alfred Everitt Orr (1886–?), For home and country. Victory liberty loan, 1918, United States Treasury, American Lithographic Co., New York [IWM PST 0256]

138: Harvey Dunn (1884–1952), They are giving all. Will you send them wheat?, 1918, United States Food Administration, W. F. Powers Litho Co., New York [IWM PST 17309]

139: Charles Livingston Bull (1874–1932), Join the Army Air Service. Be an American eagle!, 1917–18, United States Army Air Service, Alpha Litho Co. Inc., New York [IWM PST 17130]

140: J. C. Leyendecker (1874–1951), USA bonds: weapons for liberty, 1918, United States Treasury, American Lithographic Co., New York [IWM PST 4867]

141: A. W. Wurthmann, Wer die siebente kriegsanleihe zeichnet bahnt den weg (Those who subscribe to the seventh war loan clear the way), 1917, Wilhelm Jöntzen, Bremen [IWM PST 7346]

142: Paul Neumann, Der letzte hieb ist die achte kriegsanleihe (The final blow is the eighth war loan), 1918, Fritz Schneller und Co., Nürnberg [IWM PST 0457]

143: Karl Sigrist (1885–?), Zeichnet kriegsanleihe (Subscribe to the war loan), 1918, Eckstein und Stähle, Stuttgart [IWM PST 0513]

144: Willy Szesztokat (1884–1963), Schmiede das Deutsche schwert – zeichne die kriegsanleihe (Forge the German sword. Subscribe to the war loan), 1917, Wilhelm Eisfeller Graphische Kunstanstalt, Köln [IWM PST 6549]

145: A. S., Zeichnet fünfte Österreichische kriegsanleihe (Subscribe to the fifth Austrian war loan), 1916, Österreichische Länderbank [IWM PST 7646]

146: Heinrich Lefler (1863–1919), Zeichnet vierte kriegsanleihe (Subscribe to the fourth war loan), 1916, J. Weiner, Wien [IWM PST 0424]

147: Hanuš Svoboda (1878–1917), Upisujte peti Ugarski ratni zajam (Subscribe to the fifth Hungarian war loan), 1916, Hrvatska Zemaljska Banka, Melantrich, Praha [IWM PST 6712]

148: Erwin Püchinger (1876–1944), Zeichnet fünf-und-ein-halbes prozent dritte kriegsanleihe (Subscribe to the 5½ per cent third war loan), 1915, J. Weiner, Wien [IWM PST 5994]

149: Minka Podhajská (1881–1963), Zeichnet siebente kriegsanleihe! (Subscribe to the seventh war loan!), 1917, Živnostenská Banka, Der Gesellschaft für Graphische Industrie, Wien [IWM PST 3228]

150: Unknown, Travel all over the world with the Machine Gun Corps, 1919, Machine Gun Corps, H. G. B. Ltd [IWM PST 13494]

151: Alfred Leete (1882–1933), See the world and get paid for doing it, 1919, British Army, H. G. B. Ltd [IWM PST 7687]

152: Henri Gray (1858–1924), Thiepval, c.1918–19, La Compagnie du Chemin de Fer du Nord, Imprimerie Cornille et Serre, Paris [IWM PST 12805]

153: J. Seintrein, La Belgique libérée (Liberated Belgium), c.1919–20, Chemins de Fer de l'Etat Belge, Imprimerie J. E. Goossens, Bruxelles [IWM PST 3951]

154: Ludwig Hohlwein (1874–1949), Komm mit jung stahlhelm (Join us. Steel Helmet Cadet), 1920–23, Der Stahlhelm, Bund der Frontsoldaten, Hermann Sonntag und Co., München. © DACS 2007 [IWM PST 6445]

155: Julius Engelhard Ussy (1883–1964), Auch du sollst beitreten zur Reichswehr (You should join the Reich Army too), 1919, Reichswehr, Kunstanstalt Oscar Consée, München [IWM PST 6303]

156: Lina von Schauroth (1875–1970), Freikorps Hülsen (Hülsen Volunteer Corps) 1918–19, Freikorps Hülsen, J. Maubach und Co. GmbH, Frankfurt [IWM PST 2751]

157: Soldiers read posters in Barcelona calling women to arms during the Spanish Civil War, September 1936. Fox Photos/Getty Images

158: Valentin Zietara (1833–1935), Seid Einig! (Be united!), c.1918, Deutsche Vaterlandspartei (German Fatherland Party) Landesverein für das Königreich Sachsen (Regional Association for the Kingdom of Saxony), Dr Selle und Co., A-G, Berlin [IWM PST 7764]

159: Tabor and Dankó, Védd meg a proletárok hatalmát (Defend proletarian power), c.1919, Kultura Muintézet, Budapest [IWM PST 4986]

160: Glatzel, Bauet auf den Arbeiterrat und wählet Kommunistisch (Build on the Workers' Council and vote Communist), c.1919, Kommunistische Partei Österreichs (Austrian Communist Party), Druckerei M. G. I., Wien [IWM PST 7172]

161: An interior shot of a Communist Propaganda car in the 1920s, Russia. From The Mind and Face of Bolshevism: An Examination of Cultural Life in Soviet Russia, Rene Fulop-Miller (London, 1927)

162: Decoration of a public building in Russia, 1926. From The Mind and Face of Bolshevism: An Examination of Cultural Life in Soviet Russia, Rene Fulop-Miller (London, 1927)

163: Unknown, Friede, brot. Deutsche Volkspartei Bayern (Peace, bread. German People's Party in Bavaria), c.1920, Deutsche Demokratische Partei (German Democratic Party) [IWM PST 6308]

164: Lucien Bernhard (1883–1972), Die Deutsche Demokratische Partei ist die partei der frauen! (The German Democratic Party is the party of women), 1919, Deutsche Demokratische Partei (German Democratic Party), Werbedienst GmbH, Berlin W35 und München. © DACS 2007 [IWM PST 6315]

165: Arturo Ballester (1892–1981), CNT !Loor a los heroes! (Hail to the heroes!), 1936–39, Confederación Nacional del Trabajo – AIT Comite Nacional – Oficina de Información y Propaganda, Ortega, Valencia [IWM PST 8049]

166: Republican poster artists in Spain during the 1930s.

167: Heinrich Richter (1884–1981) Drei worte: ungestörte demobilmachung, aufbau der Republik, frieden (Three ideas: undisrupted demobilization, development of the Republic, peace), 1920, Nationalversammlung Wahl (National Assembly Election), Werbedienst der sozialistischen Republik, (Publicity Office of the German Socialist Republic) [IWM PST 8711]

168: Heinz Fuchs (1886–1961), Arbeiter hunger tod naht streik zerstört, arbeit ernährt tut eure pflicht arbeitet (Workers, hunger and death approach. Strikes destroy, work feeds. Do your duty, work), c.1918–19, Werbedienst der sozialistischen Republik, Publicity Office of the German Socialist Republic [IWM PST 7710]

169: Unknown, Was will Spartakus? (What does Spartakus want?), c.1919, Kommunistische Partei Deutschlands (German Communist Party), Verlag der Kommunistischen Partei Deutschlands, Berlin [IWM PST 2631]

170: Julius Engelhard Ussy (1883–1964), Bolschewismus bringt krieg, arbeitslosigkeit und hungersnot (Bolshevism brings war, unemployment and starvation), 1918, Vereinigung zur Bekämpfung des Bolschewismus (Alliance to Combat Bolshevism), Kunstanstalt Oscar Consée, München [IWM PST 5986]

171: Zehet Meyer, Wählet Kommunistisch (Vote Communist), 1920, Kommunistische Partei Österreichs (Austrian Communist Party), Druckerei M. G. I., Wien [IWM PST 5137]

172: Unknown, So war das wahlresultat 1919! Steuern – daher wählet Christlichsozial (This was the election result in 1919! Taxes. So vote Christian Socialist), 1920, Christlichsozial Partei (Christian Socialist Party) Der Gesellschaft F. R. Graphische Industrie, Wien [IWM PST 5789]

173: Bernd Steiner (1884–1933), Wählt Christlichsozial – Deutsche Christen Rettet

Österreich! (Vote Christian Socialist – German Christians. Save Austria!), c.1920, Christlichsozial Partei (Christian Socialist Party) [IWM PST 7175]

174: Lajos Szanto (1889–1965), Proletárok! Elote! Ti vagytok a világ megváltói! (Proletarians! Forward! You shall redeem the world!), c.1919, Kultura Muintézet, Budapest [IWM PST 2614]

175: Attributed to Manno Miltiades (1880–1935), Mosakodnak! (They wash themselves!), c.1919, Röttig-Romwalter Nyomda RT, Sopron [IWM PST 5960]

176: Boris M. Kustodiev (1878–1927), Freedom loan, 1917, R. Golike & A. Vilborg Association, Petrograd [IWM PST 2713]

177: Peter D. Butchkin (1886–1965), Freedom loan. War until victory, 1917, R. Golike & A. Vilborg Association, Petrograd [IWM PST 2769]

178: Unknown, The 5½ per cent military loan, 1916 [IWM PST 1646]

179: Mikhail D. Cheremnikh (1890–1962), He who is against hunger, 1920, ROSTA 36 [IWM PST 6146]

180: Unknown, For one Russia. Bolshevism has encircled the heart of Russia with a dragon, 1919, White Guard [IWM PST 2615]

181: Unknown, The Red Army. The defence of the proletarian revolution, 1919 [IWM PST 2616]

182, Unknown, What have you done for the front?, 1920 [IWM PST 6002]

183: Vesyoly, Hurrah for the great anniversary! Hurrah for the fourth Congress of the Comintern!, 1922 [IWM PST 6000]

184: J. Briones, and Jose Espert (1907–?), Izquierda Republicana al pueblo Ruso (Republican Left, the Russian people help our struggle), 1937–39, Izquierda Republicana (Republican Left), Litografía Cromo, Madrid [IWM PST 8506]

185: Unknown, Durruti. True Anarchists are against the false liberty invoked by cowards to avoid their duty, 1936–39, Rivadeneyra C. O., Madrid [IWM PST 8499]

186: Josep Renau (1907–82), El fruto del trabajo del labrador es tan sagrado para todos como el salario que recibe el obrero (The farmer's produce is as sacred as the worker's wages), 1936–39, Ministerio de Agricultura, Granjas Valencia Intervenido U.G.T. C.N.T. [IWM PST 8509]

187: Cienas, Companeros! Aumentando la producción aplastaremos el Fascismo! (Peasants! Increase production and we crush Fascism), 1936–39, Sindicato Único del Ramo de la Alimentación C.N.T. F.A.I. A.I.T., Gráfica Manen Control C.N.T. [IWM PST 8463]

188: Juan Borrás Casanova (1909–87), The Spanish workmen struggle for the liberty and culture of all countries! Solidarity with them!, 1936, Delegation de Propaganda y Prensa del CEP Valencia, Ortega, Valencia [IWM PST 8041]

189: Toledo, Las hordas Fascistas extranjeras, pretenden invadir nuestro territorio – ¡Antifascistas! Cerremosle el camino enterrandoles para siempre en nuestro suelo (The foreign Fascist hordes attempt to invade our land. Anti-Fascists! Stop their march, bury them in our soil), 1936–39, Juventud Sindicalista España, V. Mirabet UGT CNT [IWM PST 8050]

190: Pedrero, El Generalisimo (The Generalisimo), 1936–37, Junta Delegada De Defensa De Madrid, Rivadeneyra U.G.T., Madrid [IWM PST 8497]

191: Unknown, Por la España una grande y libre (For Spain, one, great and free), 1936–39, Falange Española. Jefatura Nacional de Prensa y Propaganda Seccion Mural [IWM PST 8523]

192: Unknown, España una grande libre (Spain. One, great and free), 1936–39, Falange Española. Jefatura Nacional de Prensa y Propaganda Seccion Mural, Laborde y Labayen, Tolosa [IWM PST 8828]

193: Interior view of the Office of War Information (OWI) poster 'Americans will always fight for liberty' in Union Station, Washington DC (photo Gordon Parks), 1943. Library of Congress, Prints & Photographs Division, Washington, FSA/OWI Collection [LC-USW3-018393-C]

194: Richard Klein (1890–1967), Bouwwerken in het nieuwe Duitschland (Germany's modern architecture), 1937, Reichsbahnzentrale für den Deutschen Reiseverkehr, Berlin [IWM PST 8366]

195: Unknown, Früher: arbeitsloßigheit – hoffnungsloßigheit – verwahrloßung – streik – ausßperrung. Heute: arbeiter – freude – zucht – volkskameradßchaft (Before: unemployment – hopelessness – waywardness – strike – lockout. Today: work – peace – discipline – people's comradeship) c.1934, Verantwortlich Hugo Filcher München [IWM PST 9330]

196: German boys view propaganda posters, Berlin, 1937. Photo Julien Bryan. United States Holocaust Memorial Museum, courtesy Julien Bryan

197: A poster advertising the Great Anti-Bolshevism Exhibition (Grosse Antibolschewistische Ausstellung), Nuremberg, 1937. Photo Julien Bryan. United States Holocaust Memorial Museum, courtesy Julien Bryan

198: A poster of Stalin in front of the Vienna Opera, 1945. Photo Anefo, Amsterdam. Photo collection De Brug-Djambatan, Internationaal Instituut voor Sociale Geschiedenis, Amsterdam. Courtesy Nationaal Archief, The Hague

199: Women war workers sorting rivets, Guildford, UK, 1943 [IWM Photograph Archive D 14147]

200: Ministry of Information posters, Britain, 1942 [IWM Photograph Archive D 12029]

201: Piccadilly Circus, London, 1940 [IWM Photograph Archive, D 9162]

202: G. R. Morris, Join the thrift column, 1939–45, Post Office Savings Bank [IWM PST 16427]

203: C. W. Bacon, England expects national service, 1939, Ministry of Labour and National Service HMSO, J. Weiner Ltd, London [IWM PST 13959]

204: Unknown, Dig for victory, 1939, Ministry of Agriculture, HMSO, J. Weiner Ltd [IWM PST 0059]

205: A photograph of the 'Dig for Victory' poster, Marble Arch, London [IWM Photograph Archive, D 1497]

206: Lowen, Dreams. War savings will bring them to life, 1939–45, National Savings Committee; Scottish Savings Committee [IWM PST 8298]

207: A poster warning of the dangers of venereal disease, London, 1943 [IWM Photograph Archive, D 13825]

208: Migrant fruit worker from Arkansas walking by a recruitment poster in Benton Harbor, Michigan, July 1940. Photo John Vachon

209: Unknown, We have just begun to fight!, 1943, Office of War Information, Washington DC, US Government Printing Office. Library of Congress, Prints & Photographs Division, Washington, FSA/OWI Collection [LC-USF33-T01-001906-M1] [IWM PST 0618]

210: Norman Rockwell (1894–1978), OURS … to fight for, 1943, Office of War Information, Washington DC, US Government Printing Office. Printed by permission of the Norman Rockwell Family Agency. Copyright © 1943 the Norman Rockwell Family Entities [IWM PST 2811]

211: Attributed to Harold Foster, Careless talk costs lives. Keep mum. She's not so dumb!, 1942, Ministry of Information, HMSO, Greycaine Ltd, Watford and London [IWM PST 4095]

212: Fougasse (1887–1965), Careless talk costs lives, 1942, Ministry of Information, HMSO [IWM PST 0142]

213: Oleg Savostyuk (1927–) and Boris Ouspenskiy (1927–2005), Glory to the heroes of the rear! 1941–45, 'Plakat' Publishers, Moscow [IWM PST 8419 (8)]

214: Unknown, Nuclear explosions must be prevented from turning the beautiful into monstrosities, 1987, 'Plakat' Publishers, Moscow [IWM PST 17704]

215: Unknown, In grösster not wählte Hindenburg Adolf Hitler zum Reichskanzler (In the deepest need Hindenburg chose Adolf Hitler for Reich

Chancellor), 1933, Adolf Wagner, Kunst im Druck GmbH, München [IWM PST 4956]

216: Unknown, Das ganze volk sagt am zehntes april ja! (All the people day yes on 10th April!), 1938, German Nazi Party [IWM PST 3183]

217: K. Geiss, Der arbeiter im reich des hakenkreuzes! (The worker in the swastika state!), 1932, Reinhardt Schumann Graphische Werkstätte, München [IWM PST 9329]

218: Hans Breidenstein (photograph by Dr Paul Wolff) (1887–1951), Nordseebad Norderney Presussiches staatsbad (North Sea resort Nordeney, Prussian State resort), 1937, Brönners Druckerei, Frankfurt [IWM PST 9325]

219: Ludwig Hohlwein (1874–1949), Reichsberufs wettkampf der Deutschen jungend (Reichs vocational competition for German youth), 1934, Chromo Lithographische Kunstanstalt AG, München. © DACS 2007 [IWM PST 9328]

220: Ludwig Hohlwein (1874–1949), Im bund Deutscher mädel – Reichssporttag des BDM (Reichs sports day for the League of German Maidens), 1934, Chromo Lithographische Kunstanstalt AG, München. © DACS 2007 [IWM PST 9337]

221: Hermann Witte, Baut jugendherberge und heime (Build youth hostels and homes), 1938, Verband Deutscher Jugendherbergen (the Association of German Youth Hostels), Druck Langebartels und Jurgens, Altona [IWM PST 3172]

222: Hermann Witte, Wir brauchen jugendherbergen (We need youth hostels), 1938, Verband Deutscher Jugendherbergen (the Association of German Youth Hostels), Druck Langebartels und Jurgens, Altona [IWM PST 9332]

223: Franz Würbel (1896–?) Gesunde eltern – gesunde kinder! (Healthy parents – healthy children), 1933, Nationalsozialistische Deutsche Arbeiterpartei Nationalsozialistische Volkswohlfahrt (National Socialist People's Welfare), Reichsfuhrung, Berlin [IWM PST 8517]

224: Abepy, Juden komplott gegen Europa! (Jewish conspiracy against Europe!), 1942, Jan Acke, Filips van den Elzaslaan, Kortrijk [IWM PST 8359]

225: Unknown, A Teraz Oczekiwaloby to i Was (And now the same fate would have awaited you), 1942, published by the Nazis in Poland and the Ukraine [IWM PST 8342]

226: Venabert, Assez! Ici repose un soldat Français mort pour La Patrie (Enough! Here lies a French soldier who died for the Mother Country), 1942, Ligue Française, Bedos et Cie Imprimeurs, Paris [IWM PST 8358]

227: Unknown, Avec l'ouvrier soldat pour le socialisme (With the worker a soldier for socialism), c.1942, O. Platteau und Co., Antwerpen [IWM PST 6483]

228: M. M., Stand up to fight Bolshevism in the ranks of the Galicia division, 1944, ZKW Druckereibetrieb II, Lemberg [IWM PST 8328]

229: Unknown, Nederlanders: voor uw eer en geweten op! Tegen het Bolsjewisme (Netherlanders: for your honour and conscience! Against Bolshevism),1943, Waffen-SS Dienststelle des Reichskommissars [IWM PST 6431]

230: Unknown, Uw plaats is nog vrij in de Waffen SS (Your place is still vacant in the Waffen SS), 1942, Waffen SS Dienststelle des Reichskommissars [IWM PST 9199]

231: Attributed to Raoul Eric Castel, En travaillant en Allemagne tu seras l'ambassadeur de la qualité Française (While working in Germany you will be the ambassador of French quality), 1943, Office de Répartition de l'Affichage, Bedos et Cie Imprimeurs, Paris [IWM PST 3321]

232: Attributed to Lucas, The British Commonwealth of Nations. Together, 1939–45, HMSO, J. Weiner Ltd, London [IWM PST 8457]

233: Unknown, Let us go forward together, 1940, J. Weiner Ltd, London [IWM PST 14971]

234: F. H. K. Henrion (1914–90), We're in it together, 1943, HMSO, Henry Hildesley Ltd, London [IWM PST 10019]